WALKER EVANS	DAVID GOLDBLATT	
1903 – 1975	*1930	
ANDREAS FEININGER	BERND / HILLA BECHER	
1906 – 1999	1931 – 2007 / 1934 – 2015	
HENRI CARTIER-BRESSON	BRUCE DAVIDSON	
1908 – 2004	*1933	
WILLY RONIS	RENÉ BURRI	
1910 – 2009	1933 – 2014	
ROBERT DOISNEAU	LEE FRIEDLANDER	
1912 – 1994	*1934	
ROBERT CAPA	MALICK SIDIBÉ	
1913 – 1954	1936 – 2016	
HELMUT NEWTON	JOSEF KOUDELKA	
1920 – 2004	*1938	
DIANE ARBUS	SEBASTIÃO SALGADO	
1923 – 1971	*1944	
RICHARD AVEDON	ROBERT MAPPLETHORPE	
1923 – 2004	1946 – 1989	
SEYDOU KEÏTA	HIROSHI SUGIMOTO	
1923 – 2001	*1948	
ROBERT HÄUSSER	KAVEH GOLESTAN	
*1924	1950 – 2003	
ARA GÜLER	MARTIN PARR	
*1928	*1952	
GARRY WINOGRAND	NAN GOLDIN	
1928 – 1984	*1953	
WILLIAM KLEIN	ANDREAS GURSKY	WOLFGANG TILLMANS
*1928	*1955	*1968

1900 – 1920s	1930 – 1950s	1960s

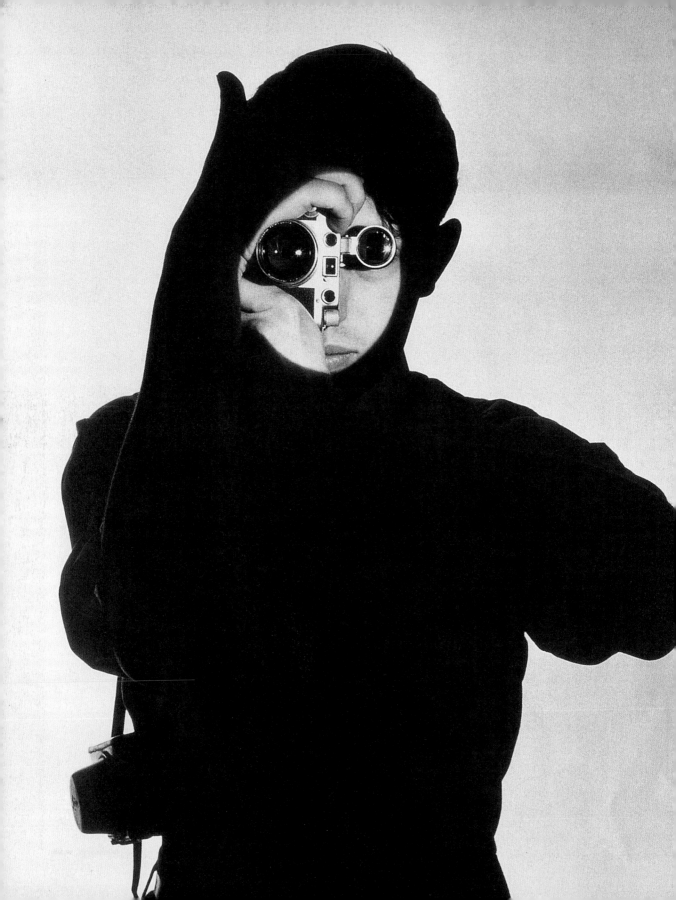

50 PHOTOGRAPHERS

YOU SHOULD KNOW

Peter Stepan

PRESTEL

Munich · London · New York

CONTENTS

01

JULIA MARGARET CAMERON

She turned women into Madonnas and children into allegories of love or charity. But it was the aesthetic quality of her works that assured her lasting fame as the first great woman photographer.

JULIA MARGARET CAMERON

1815 Born in Calcutta, British India

1818–1834 Numerous visits to Europe, especially France, where she is largely educated

1842 Sees her first photographs, sent to Calcutta by John Herschel

1848 She and her husband move from Ceylon (Sri Lanka) to England

1864 Takes up photography, becoming a member of several photographic societies

1865 Exhibitions of her works in London, Berlin and Dublin; a number are acquired by the South Kensington Museum

1874 Publication of Tennyson's *Idylls of the King* with 13 photos by Cameron

1875 She and her husband move back to Ceylon, where she photographs servants and workers

1879 Dies in Ceylon

It was not until the age of 48, and after raising six children, that Julia Margaret Cameron took up photography. Back then this was still a laborious activity, involving cumbersome apparatus, glass plates, and difficult chemical processes. Viewing commercial visiting-card portraits as "vulgar, leveling, and literal," Cameron suffused her portraits of relatives or illustrious friends with an aura of piety. A scene with a sleeping child and adults became Christ's birth in Bethlehem; two women with a lily became an Annunciation. She called a girl with billowing hair, taken in profile, *The Angel at the Tomb*. The model, as so often, was Cameron's maid, Mary Hillier. Yet Cameron made no attempt to re-create scenes from the Holy Land historically, with the aid of props or oriental costumes. It was her unconventionally familiar, indeed intimate, treatment of her soberly dressed models that infused her idyllic images with poetry.

Over a third of Cameron's photographs are portraits of women—earnestly gazing from heavy-lidded, soulful eyes as if yearning for a land of beauty. They have the sultry melancholy of the figures of Edward Burne-Jones and Dante Gabriel Rossetti, to whom Cameron made a present of 40 of her pictures. And like the Pre-Raphaelites, she was fascinated by Italian Renaissance art. The titles of her pictures of women with children were themselves a pure homage to Raphael: *La Madonna Adolorata*, *La Madonna della Ricordanza*, *La Madonna Aspettante*. A portrait of a lady with a musical instrument was inspired by Raphael's *St. Cecilia* in Bologna; the portraits of women holding lilies were reminiscent of Perugino or Francia. Yet Cameron also alluded to ancient mythology: her portraits of little Freddy Gould became *The Young Astyanax* (1866) or *The Young Endymion* (1873).

In 1875, Cameron illustrated *Idylls of the King and Other Poems* by Alfred Lord Tennyson, the popular Victorian poet and her sometime neighbor on the Isle of Wight. Unlike her religious subjects, she now resorted to elaborate costumes and settings to evoke the legend of King Arthur, around which Tennyson's poems revolved. Sir Lancelot in chain mail, Queen Guinevere, Vivien and Merlin stepped out to face the audience, as if on stage. As Cameron once described her credo, "My aspirations are to ennoble Photography and to secure for it the character and uses of High Art by combining the Real and Ideal and sacrificing nothing of the Truth by all possible devotion to Poetry and Beauty."

Cameron also created a series of significant portraits, her sitters including the astronomer John F.W. Herschel, Henry Taylor, Thomas Carlyle, Gustave Doré, William Holman Hunt, and Charles Darwin. In a space of only 15 years she produced an extensive photographic oeuvre, of which over 1,200 images have survived.

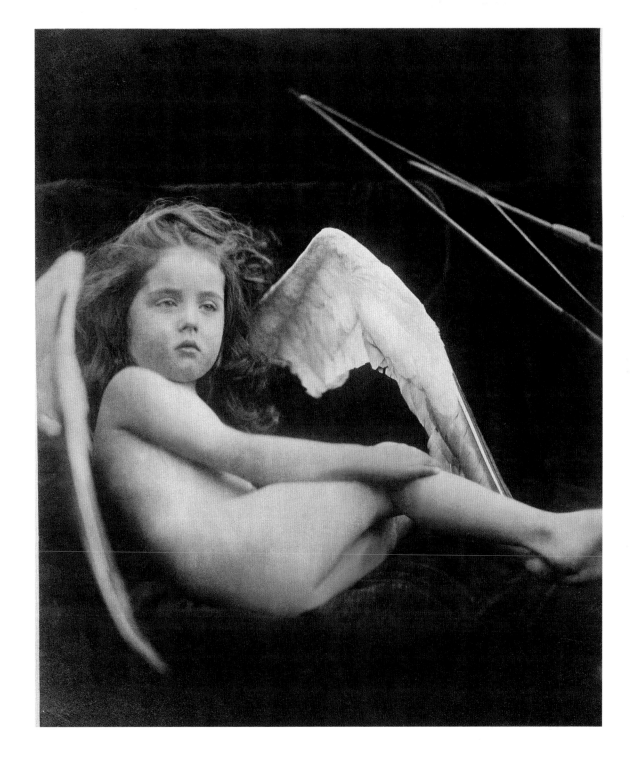

Cupid, 1872

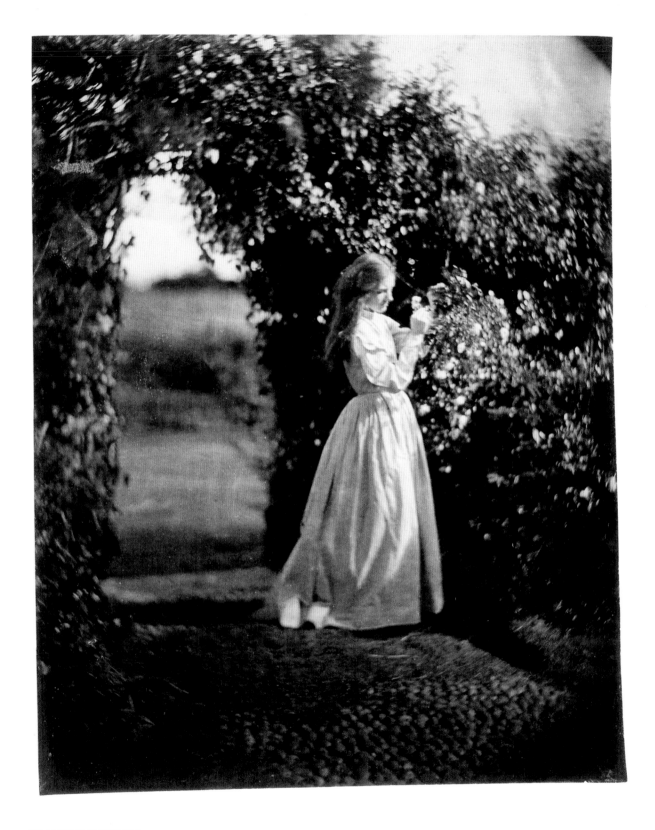

The Gardener's Daughter, 1867

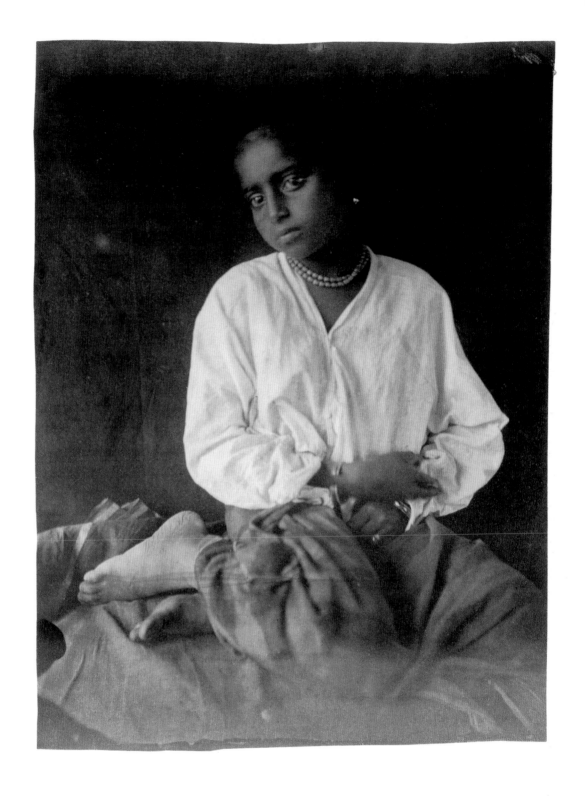

Girl, Ceylon, 1875–1879

02

FÉLIX NADAR

Félix Nadar was a man of many parts: well-known journalist, novelist, and caricaturist as well as a photraprapher who created striking images of the famous. He also took photos from a balloon and in the Paris catacombs.

FÉLIX NADAR

Félix Nadar was one of the most creative, original and daring artists and entrepreneurs of the 19th century. When he was a young man, his socialist sympathies caused him to be placed under police surveillance. He fought duels when honor demanded, and was likely befriended with more writers and artists than anyone else at the time. Nadar nursed the dying Charles Baudelaire, who called him "the most astonishing expression of vitality," and hosted the Impressionists' first exhibition on his premises. Nadar supported the old and impoverished Honoré Daumier by helping to organize a show of his works. It was Daumier who made the famous caricature of the aviation pioneer in his balloon, "raising photography to the level of art" (1862). Nadar operated a private balloon called "Le Géant" (The Giant), and in face of the impending French defeat by the Prussians in 1870 he and his friends established a "Company of Military Balloon Aviators" to conduct aerial reconnaissance.

After taking up photography in 1854, not a year passed before Nadar produced now legendary photographs: the experiments with electrophysiological facial distortions conducted by Dr. Duchenne de Boulogne (with Nadar's brother, Adrien Tournachon, as co-photographer), and portraits of the great mime Charles Debureau, who reinterpreted the Commedia dell'Arte role of Pierrot. Nadar had hired Debureau for a series of "expressive heads" to promote his new studio. These pictures by the brothers—collectively billed as "Nadar jeune"—won a First Class medal at the 1855 Paris World's Fair. Yet sadly a quarrel over rights ensued between Félix and Adrien that would occupy the courts for a long time.

The name Nadar stood above all for high quality portraiture. His *Panthéon Nadar* immortalized the intellectual greats of the day: artists such as Doré, Daumier, Delacroix, Millet, Daubigny, Courbet, Manet, Monet, and Rodin; authors such as George Sand, Marceline Desbordes-Valmore, Charles Baudelaire, Dumas, and Hugo; and composers such as Hector Berlioz, Rossini, Offenbach, and Verdi.

Many of these portraits have since become canonical records of their sitters' appearance. The straightforward yet monumental style of the portraits, the way they bring out the sitters' intellect and charisma, not to mention humor, and underplay their attire and surroundings, made Nadar famous. These were portraits of artists by an artist.

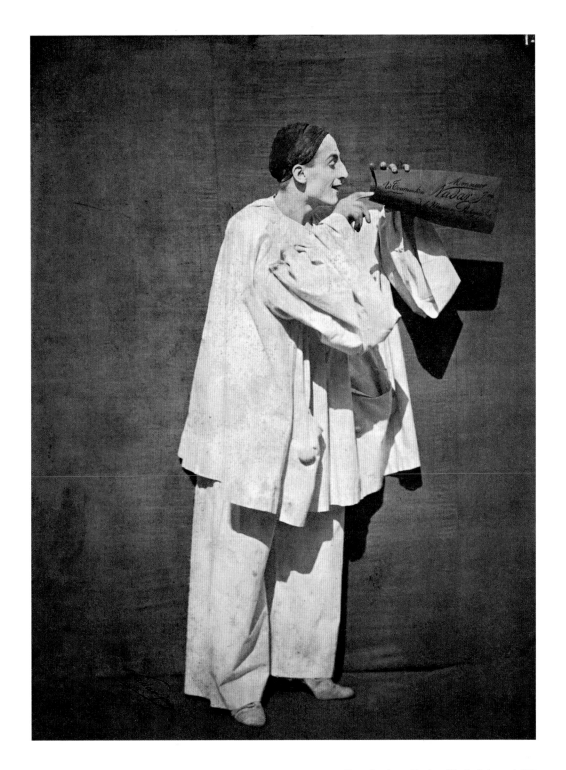

Pierrot Opening an Envelope (Charles Debureau), 1855

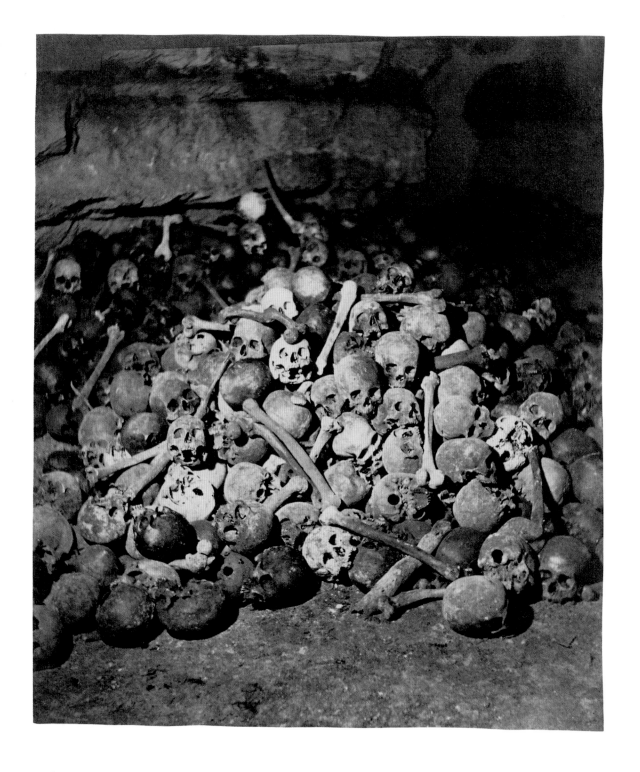

Catacombs of Paris, Crypt 8, 1861–1862

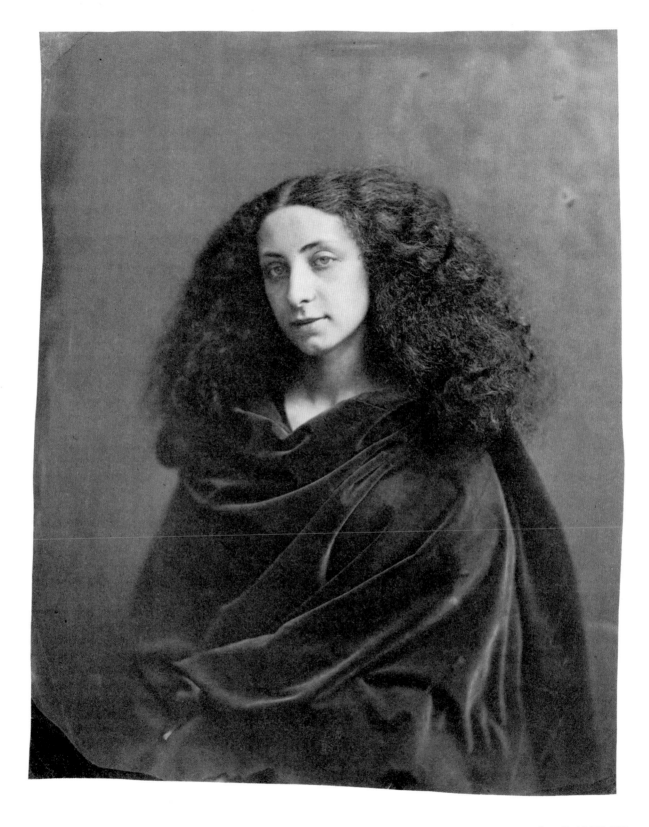

Young Model, 1861–1862

03

MATHEW BRADY

Though Mathew Brady seldom stood behind a camera himself, he was the brilliant impresario of a project that for the first time in history conveyed the true horrors of the battlefield.

MATHEW BRADY

Although the Englishman Roger Fenton had already sent pictures from the front lines—in the Crimean War—a few years previously, neither his nor Brady's Civil War images represented war photography as we now know it. Due to long exposure times and complicated chemical processes, Brady was hardly ever able to capture a battle in progress. He recorded the before and after phases, but when the bullets began to fly, the medium of photography—barely a quarter century after its invention—was still too slow. Brady's archive contains pictures of forts, trenches, cannon and mortars, arsenals and covered wagon parks. We see the armored ships and side-wheel steamers of the Federal Navy, but not the battles they fought in the harbors and at sea. Instead, there is portrait after portrait of groups and individuals: the battalions and crews on deck, the officers, generals, and, finally, President Abraham Lincoln visiting the troops. Hardly has the infantry marched in with fixed bayonets when the men lie dead on the ground. These are the most harrowing images of all—the bodies of Confederate and Union troops littering the battlefields of Antietam, Maryland, and Gettysburg, Pennsylvania.

And then the bombed and shelled Richmond, Virginia. This was the seat of the Confederate high command, who shortly before abandoning it blew up the powder stores, devastating the center of town. Not until the uprising of the Paris Commune in 1871 would such ghostly ruins be photographed again.

The Scotsman Alexander Gardner (1821–1882), originally business manager of Brady's Washington branch, worked for him only during the first year of the War of Secession. After a quarrel over the rights to his pictures, he set up shop on his own. Gardner's work as Photographer to the Army of the Potomac culminated in 1866 with a two-volume documentation, *Gardner's Photographic Sketch Book of the War*. Nearly half of its photographs were actually taken by Timothy O'Sullivan (ca. 1840–1882), a former apprentice in Brady's studio, who entered Gardner's employ in 1862–1863.

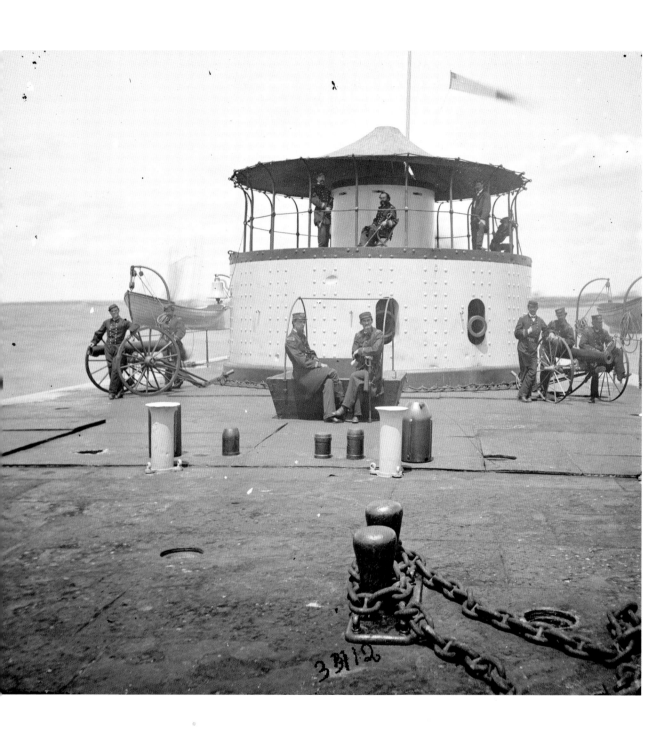

Charleston Harbor, South Carolina, Deck and Officers of USS Monitor Catskill. Photographer unidentified

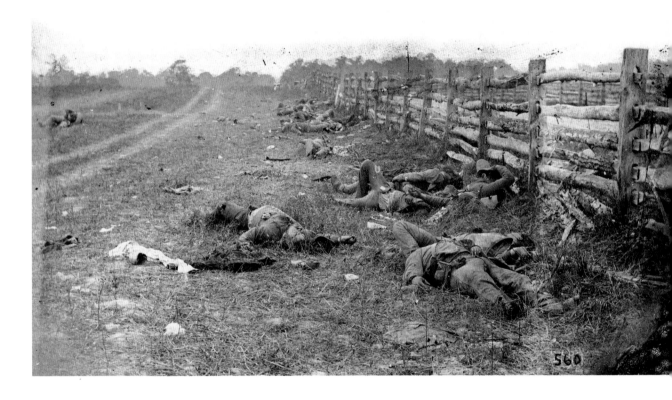

Confederate dead on the Hagerstown Road, Antietam, Maryland, September 1862. Photographer Alexander Gardner

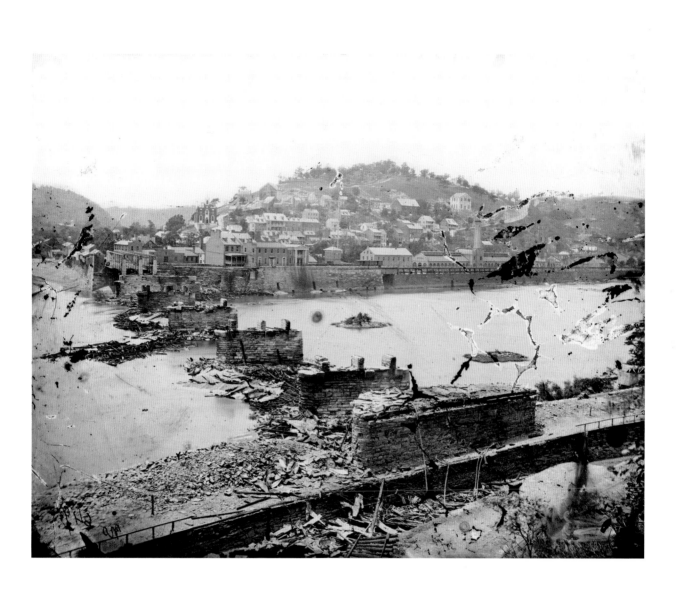

Ruins of Railroad Bridge, Harper's Ferry, West Virginia, September–October 1862. Photographer C.O. Bostwick

04 EADWEARD JAMES MUYBRIDGE

Entrepreneur and inventor, Muybridge is best known for his photos of animals and people in motion, which added an entirely new dimension to photography.

EADWEARD JAMES MUYBRIDGE

It was with a one-month expedition to the Yosemite Valley in California, then still a god-forsaken area, that Muybridge first drew attention to himself. One commentator praised his pictures, "taken from points of view not heretofore used ... climbing to the best points of sight with his camera, often with great difficulty and danger ... 800 pictures, some of which present effects beyond any heretofore taken." These Yosemite pictures marked the beginning of Muybridge's career as a government photographer. One of their much-praised features seems almost banal today: skies full of fluffy clouds combined with a detailed landscape foreground. Muybridge frequently employed the montage technique, permitting him to manipulate landscape photographs such that, for instance, they appeared to have been taken by moonlight.

His major achievement, however, required more than a few darkroom tricks. In order to record a horse in full gallop, an exposure time of less than 1/1000 second was necessary. How was this to be done in an epoch when glass plates still had to be exposed in a wet-collodion process for at least ten seconds, if not several minutes? Muybridge, with John D. Isaacs, worked untiringly on improving shutters and light-sensitive emulsions, and in 1877 finally succeeding in making a few instantaneous photographs of the horse Occident in full canter. To his contemporaries, this seemed as sensational as breaking the sound barrier would decades later.

In consequence, Muybridge envisioned recording the sequential movements of animals, and later of human beings, with the aid of entire batteries of cameras—first 12, then 24—and sophisticated systems of electrical contacts. The experiments consumed great sums of money, initially provided by Muybridge's patrons, former Governor Stanford, and later the University of Pennsylvania. In 1887, his legendary work *Animal Locomotion* appeared. According to an announcement, the 781 phototypes in 11 volumes contained "more than 20,000 figures of men, women, and children, animals and birds, actively engaged in walking, galloping, flying, working, jumping, fighting ... which illustrate motion or the play of muscles." This encyclopedia remains a must for physiologists and those fascinated by images, a feast for the eye.

Muybridge's inventiveness knew no bounds. In a letter to the editor of 1882, he was the first to suggest the idea of photographing the finishes of horse races in order to exclude judges' errors. Muybridge also made panoramic photographs 26 feet long and was the first to photograph a solar eclipse.

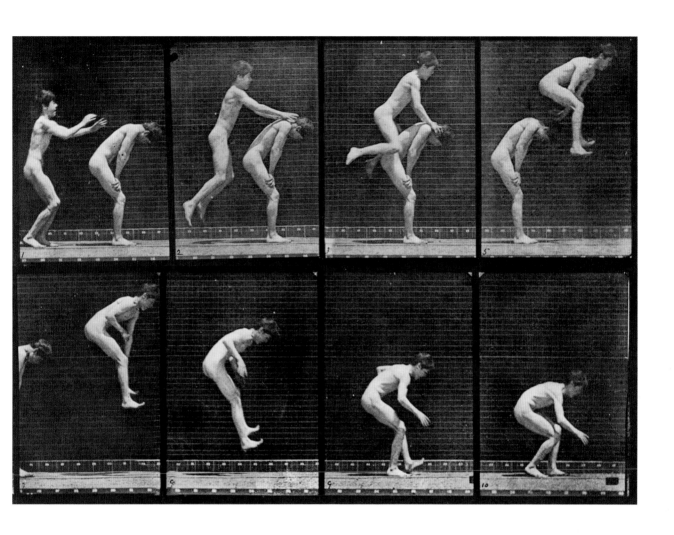

Jumping Over a Boy's Back (Leapfrog), 1887

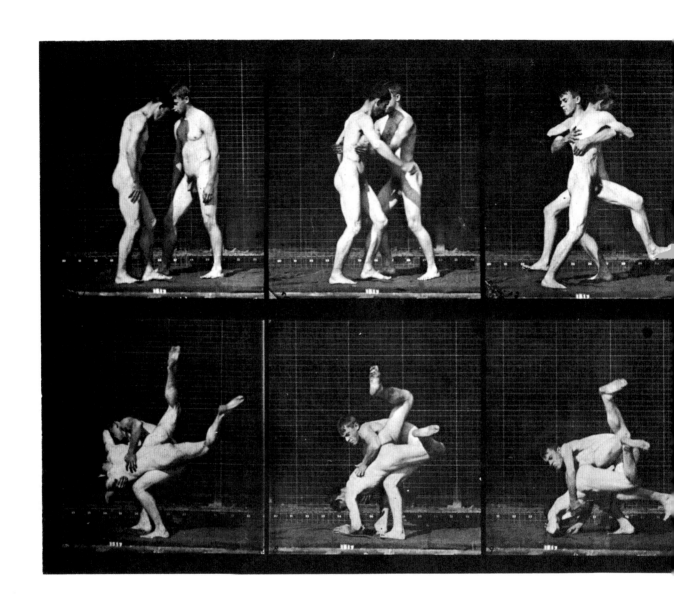

Wrestling, Graeco-Roman, 1887

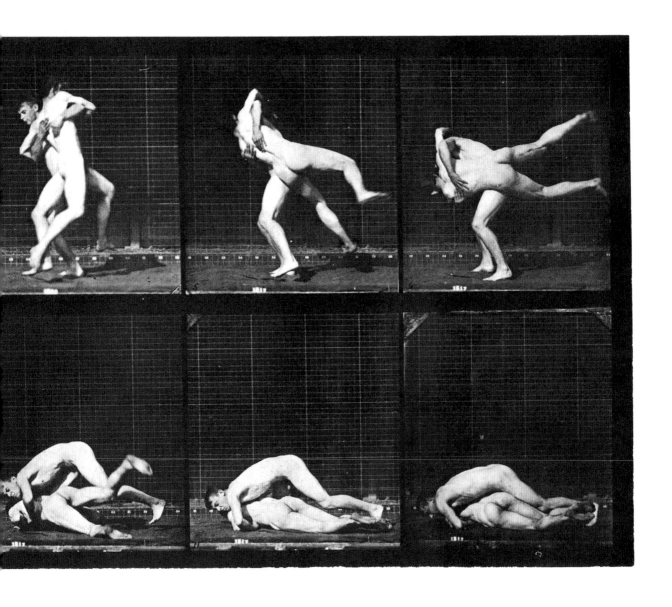

05

FELICE BEATO

A 19th-century Robert Capa, Felice Beato recorded several wars. Widely traveled, he also took the earliest photographs of architectural monuments in Palestine, India, China, and Japan.

FELICE BEATO

ca. 1834 Born in Venice

1855 Documents the Crimean War

1860 Records the end of the second Opium War in China; meets Charles Wirgman, illustrator for the *Illustrated London News*

1861 Offers his negatives for sale in London, but with little success

1863 Opens a studio in the foreigners' district of Yokohama, Japan

1864 Documents the Shimonoseki Retribution Campaign

1866 Studio destroyed by fire

1868 Two-volume *Photographic Views of Japan*

1877 Sells his studio, complete with negatives

1885 Records the British campaign in Sudan

1889 Opens a studio in Burma

1907–1908 Dies in Rangoon, Burma

His reputation was established by pictures from Crimea, "photographic views and panoramas" of the Indian Mutiny, and of architecture in cities such as Lucknow, Cawnpore, Delhi, Agra, Benares and the province of Punjab. Not to forget the bone-strewn site of the British massacre at Lucknow (1857). In the last year of the Opium War, Felice Beato was named official photographic reporter. With his shots of Taku in eastern China after it was taken by the English and French on August 21, 1860, he provided—just a year before Brady's pictures of the American Civil War—a shocking scene of colonial war: numerous dead bodies on the ramps and positions inside the North Fort. After the capture of Peking a few weeks later, Beato documented the stormed walls and gates, and produced multipartite panoramas of the bastions and the city. Seemingly even more significant in retrospect is his documentation of a great range of buildings, including royal palaces, temples, pagodas, gates and sepulchers, Lamaistic temples, and Islamic mosques. A major art historical record is Beato's image of the Imperial Summer Palace, torched by the British on October 18 in retribution for the killing of 20 British soldiers in Chinese custody.

Hardly had the Japanese harbor city of Yokohama been opened to Europeans when Beato and his partner established a photographic studio there. He produced the period's finest views of Japan, including panoramas of the cities and harbors of Nagasaki and Yokohama. Beato began photographing Edo (now Tokyo) half a century before it became the new Japanese capital. He portrayed the Dutch and American legations, members of the European colony over tea, on Queen Victoria's birthday, at the races, rowing, and hunting. In 1866, with the Dutch consul general, he climbed Fujiyama, but was unable to take pictures of the summit.

Incomparable are Beato's photographs of Japanese "native types," representatives of occupations and ordinary people of the kind you would meet on the street—from coolies and tattooed stable boys to itinerant priests, from fishmongers to saké purveyors. Especially picturesque are the Kando fencers and the Samurai warriors, whose heyday had passed with the onset of the Meiji period. One of the four Japanese painters who tinted Beato's prints is also portrayed, wearing eyeglasses and with brush at the ready. Then there are the everyday scenes, a doctor with his patient, views of an antique shop, officers drinking tea. In genre pictures, Beato captured women applying makeup, and geishas smoking opium or playing music. It was especially Europeans who lived in Japan or were traveling through who bought such pictures from Beato. In 1868 he collected them in a two-volume work, *Photographic Views of Japan*.

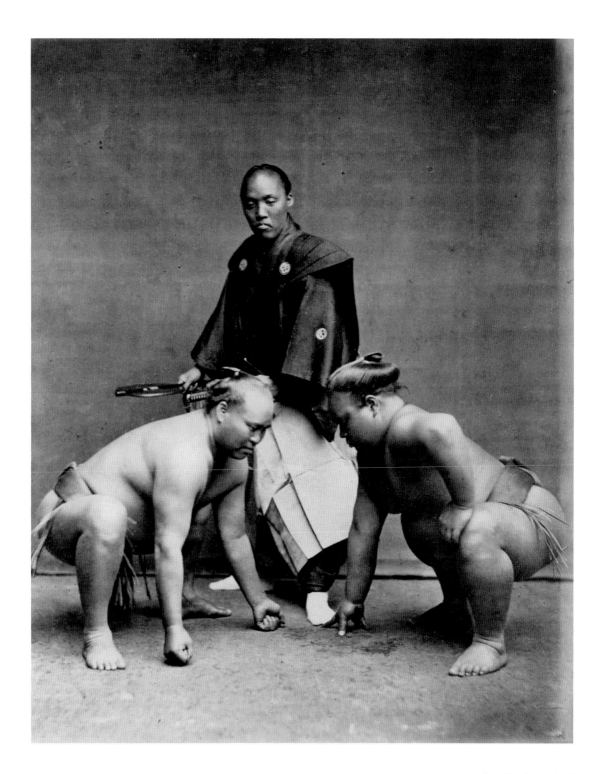

Sumo Wrestlers, undated

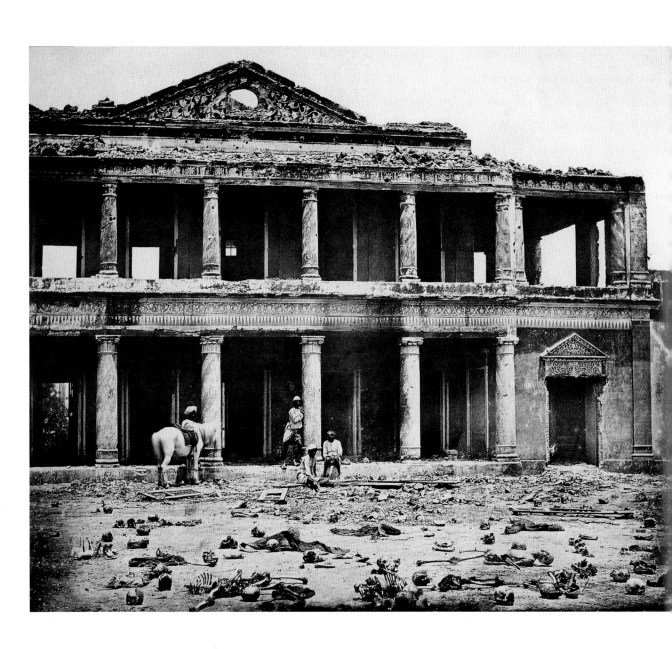

Interior of the Secundra Bagh after the Slaughter of 2,000 Rebels by the 93rd Highlanders and 4th Punjab Regiment, Lucknow, November 1857

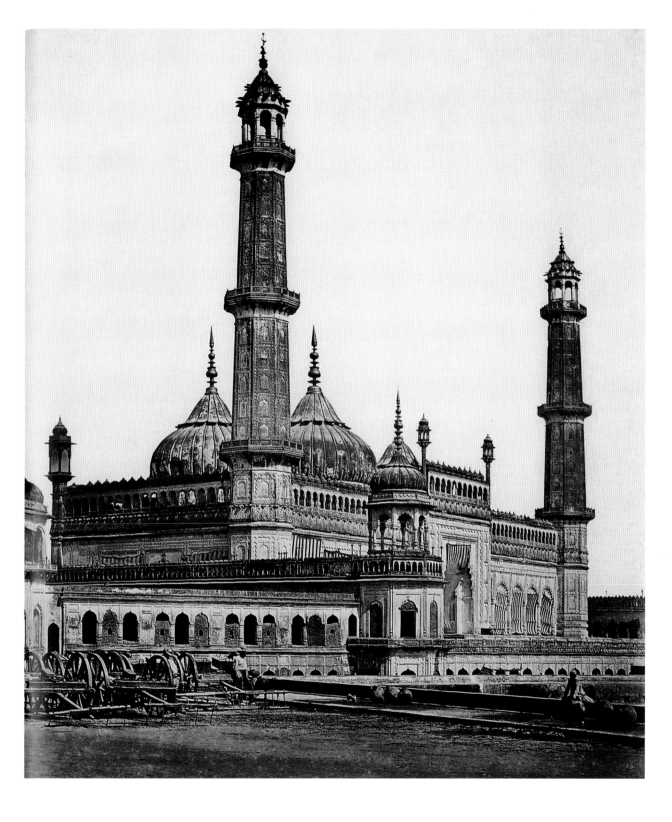

Mosque Inside Asophoo Dowlah's Emambara, Lucknow, 1857

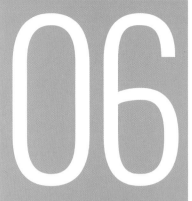

06

EUGÈNE ATGET

Eugène Atget's photographs—about 10,000 urban and rural views made over almost 40 years—amount to the most extensive and coherent archive of Old Paris and Old France in existence.

EUGÈNE ATGET

1857 Born in Libourne, France

1879 Trains as an actor but is forced to break off his studies

1883–1888 Works as an itinerant actor

1888 Begins to take photographs with a plate camera (18 x 24 cm)

1890 Opens a shop for photo aids

1897 Begins a "collection of photographic views of Old Paris"

1907–1912 Photographs areas of Paris, and documents the Tuileries for the Bibliothèque Historique de la Ville de Paris

1910 Series on fortifications and shops for the Bibliothèque Nationale

1917–1918 Work interrupted by WWI

1919 Resumes work

1922 Begins to work in a freer style

1920 Les Monuments Historiques acquires 2,600 glass negatives

1927 Dies in Paris

His views of villages and Paris in the early modern period were neither official nor representative. Picturesque farmsteads and village squares, old wells and wisteria climbing flaking house walls apparently interested him more than imposing façades. A freshly plowed field, a bare tree, a street flanked by windowless walls—such subjects were more to Atget's taste. Without artfully composing what he saw or charging it with atmosphere, he let things be as they were. And were it not for the sonorous sepia that suffuses the old prints with a nostalgic mood, many of his works might figure as textbook examples of "straight photography." It was things and places—houses, streets, plants that intrigued him, and his pictures rarely show human life directly. Atget went out very early in the morning, or used such long exposure times that chance passersby vanished from the image, or appear as ghost-like smudges.

Atget's Paris is a metropolis of sun-drenched courtyards and lanes, old bridges, and barges silently passing by. For the Bibliothèque Historique de la Ville de Paris and the Bibliothèque Nationale—his most important patrons—the École des Beaux Arts, the Union des Arts Décoratifs, and the Victoria and Albert Museum, he recorded city blocks, buildings, elegant interiors, and stairwells, or architectural details such as portals, door knockers, even the details of a stucco decoration. Other series of works were devoted to wrought-iron grilles and balustrades, or the popular signs over the entrances to bistros. The Paris of the grand boulevards was not Atget's Paris.

Unlike the work of many other photographers, Atget's shows barely any stylistic change, being apparently immune to changing fashions. At most, one or the other courtyard picture might seem to contain an echo of concurrent Cubism, or a photograph like *Porte de Bercy, sortie du PLM* (1913) to exhibit a Constructivist bent. The displays in the Paris shop windows he recorded would be unthinkable without the *retour à l'ordre* (return to order) of the 1920s or the Surrealist mystique of objects. Man Ray indeed reproduced four of these images in *La Révolution surrealiste* (1926).

The documentary photographs were supplemented with pictures of representatives of the "petits métiers"—a door-to-door lampshade salesman, a baker, a postman, a hurdy-gurdy man accompanied by a singer. In Versailles, Atget captured women waiting for customers outside a brothel. And then there is his picture of asphalt workers (1899–1900), which spirits us back for a moment into the social reality of France over a century ago.

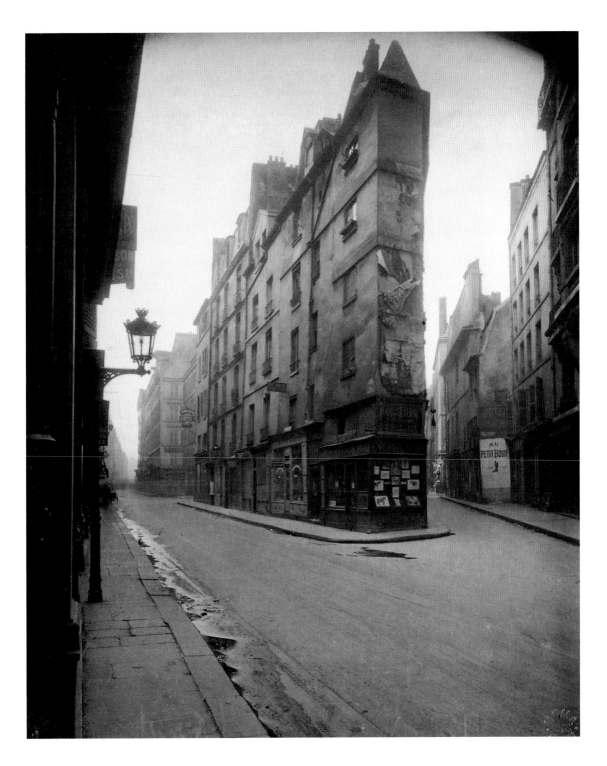

A Corner, Rue de Seine, May 1924

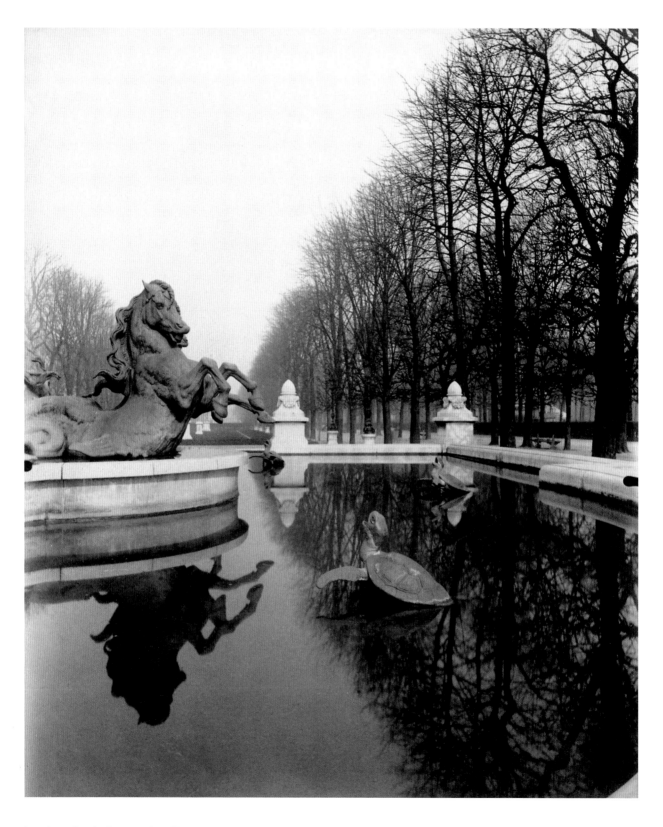

Luxembourg, Fontaine Carpeaux, 1901–1902

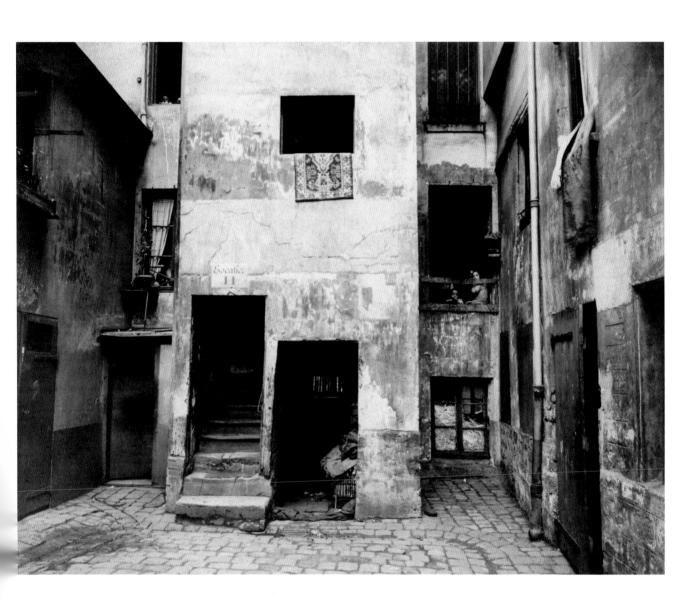

Courtyard, Rue Broca 41, 1912

07

ALFRED STIEGLITZ

Alfred Stieglitz played a major role in introducing modernism to the United States, and in making photography accepted as an art form there decades before anywhere else.

ALFRED STIEGLITZ

Stieglitz belonged to the generation of photographers who thought their art was greatly underestimated. By means of literary subject matter, a picturesque, atmospheric style, and elaborate printing techniques, he and his friends attempted to rival painting. Stieglitz's great pioneering act was the founding of the journal *Camera Work*, a forum for avant-garde photography from 1903 to 1917, and at the same time also a window on modern European art. Great care was devoted to reproducing the photographs, in heliogravure on Japan paper, prints that Stieglitz and his friend and co-photographer Edward Steichen viewed as original graphic works. Despite occasionally overly symbolic titles, such as *The Hand of Man* (1903), the Stieglitz images published in *Camera Work* were surprisingly modern: locomotives surrounded by power lines against an urban backdrop, New York street scenes with horse-drawn carriages, crowded ferries. The city in snow or rain, clouds of steam pouring from ships' stacks and chimneys, held a special attraction for him. With his epoch-making photograph *The Steerage* (1907), Stieglitz finally said farewell to atmospheric impressionism.

When in 1905 his friend Steichen moved to a larger apartment, making his previous one at 291 Fifth Avenue available, the success story of Stieglitz's Little Galleries of the Photo Secession, later known simply as the "291" gallery, began. An ad of the time promised "Permanent Exhibitions (November-April) of Pictorial Photographs—American, Viennese, German, French, British—as well as of modern art not necessarily photographic..."

The culmination of Stieglitz's work came in the 1920s with *Equivalents*, studies of a horizonless sky over Lake George with clouds appearing in ever-changing formations and textures. Here his penchant for painterly effects was subsumed in a form in which the individual image became a variation in an extended sequence of formal studies. Synesthesia provided inspiration: Stieglitz called the first results *Music–A Sequence of Ten Cloud Photographs*.

Lake George would become the site of his photographic homage to Georgia O'Keeffe. Between 1917 and 1936, Stieglitz took about 350 pictures of his lover, a collection ranging from intimate, highly stylized portraits to images of her hands, and nude studies. When a selection of the latter was shown for the first time in 1921, it touched off a storm of indignation.

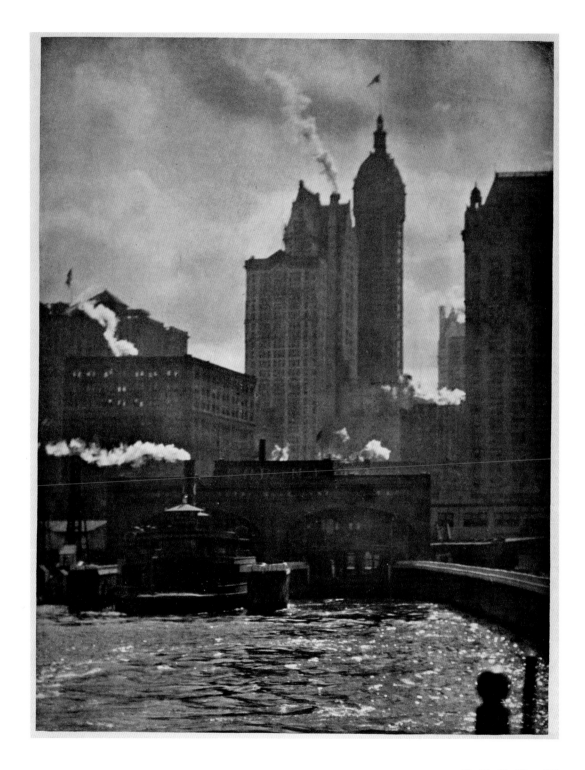

The City of Ambitions, 1910

08 EDWARD SHERIFF CURTIS

Edward Sheriff Curtis focused on the world of Native Americans, documenting a fast-disappearing way of life and its often charismatic personalities.

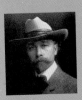

EDWARD SHERIFF CURTIS

1868 Born in Whitewater, Wisconsin

1885 Begins apprentice in St Paul, Minnesota

1887 Family moves to Seattle, Washington; becomes joint proprietor of a photographic studio

1895 First portrait of a Native American

1896 Moves to Seattle

1900 Joins an expedition to the Blackfeet in Montana

1907–1930 *The North American Indian*, with 40,000 images of more than 80 ethnic groups

1915 Book and film, *Indian Days of the Long Ago*

1922 Opens studio in Los Angeles, and works for Hollywood film studios

1924 Sells rights to his film *In the Land of the Head-Hunters* to the American Museum of Natural History

1927 Travels to Alaska

1952 Dies in Los Angeles

Edward S. Curtis followed in the footsteps of the great painter of Native Americans George Catlin, who, after beginning to visit indigenous tribes in 1832, spent many years recording their religious rites and hunting expeditions, and making individual portraits. His famous "Gallery of the Indians" was widely exhibited in North America and Europe. After that, it was a new invention, photography, with which the demise of the old ways was increasingly recorded. From the end of the Civil War in 1865 to Wounded Knee, the final conflict between Native Americans and Europeans in 1890, most photographs of tribes were taken during visits of delegations to Washington and in connection with large geographic and geological surveys conducted in the 1860s and 1870s. Various "shadow catchers" provided newspaper images and photographic shows on the East Coast. Curtis took his first portrait of a Native American in 1895, and in 1898 he was invited by anthropologist George Bird Grinnell to join an expedition to the Blackfeet in Montana.

By the time Curtis began to capture "the face of the Indians," their rich culture was long a thing of the past. The majority lived on reservations, wore European clothing, and had abandoned their old customs. Still, Curtis made one last, unprecedented attempt to create a grand panorama of Native American life. He devoted 30 years to this monumental project, publishing it from 1907 to 1930 in 20 volumes under the title *The North American Indian*. From the deserts of Mexico to Alaska, he visited over 80 ethnic groups west of the Mississippi, to record their daily life, religious rites, and leading personalities. Fishing and hunting scenes, women cooking, making pots or weaving, and a range of artistic artifacts—innumerable facets of the lives of children, adolescents and adults were reflected in Curtis's imagery. The charm of the exotic, especially the elaborate traditional costumes on which earlier artists and photographers had focused, made way for an interest in the individual character of faces. Many pictures nevertheless seem to reflect an attempt to revive earlier, lost customs.

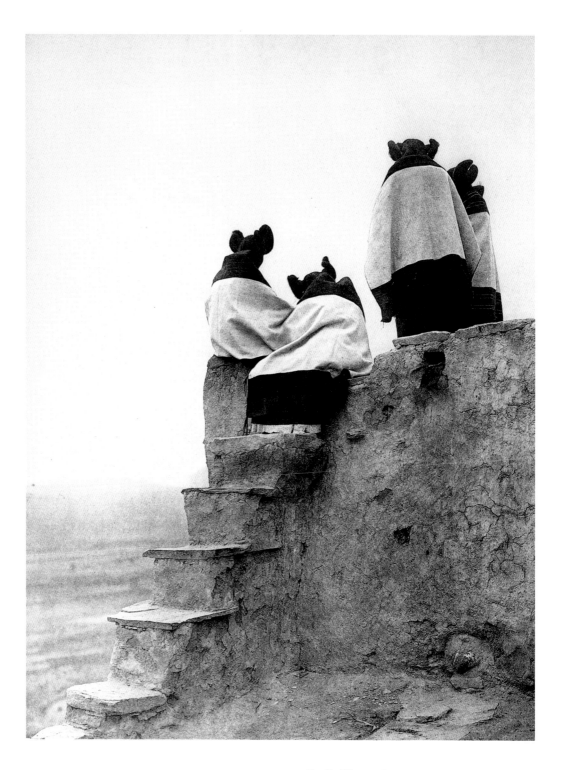

Four Hopi Women at Top of Adobe Steps, New Mexico, ca. 1906

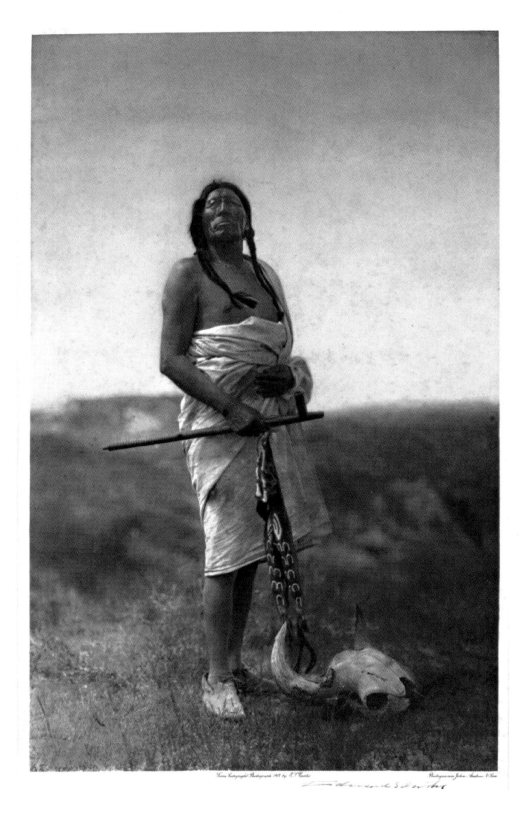

The Medicine Man (Slow Bull), ca. 1907

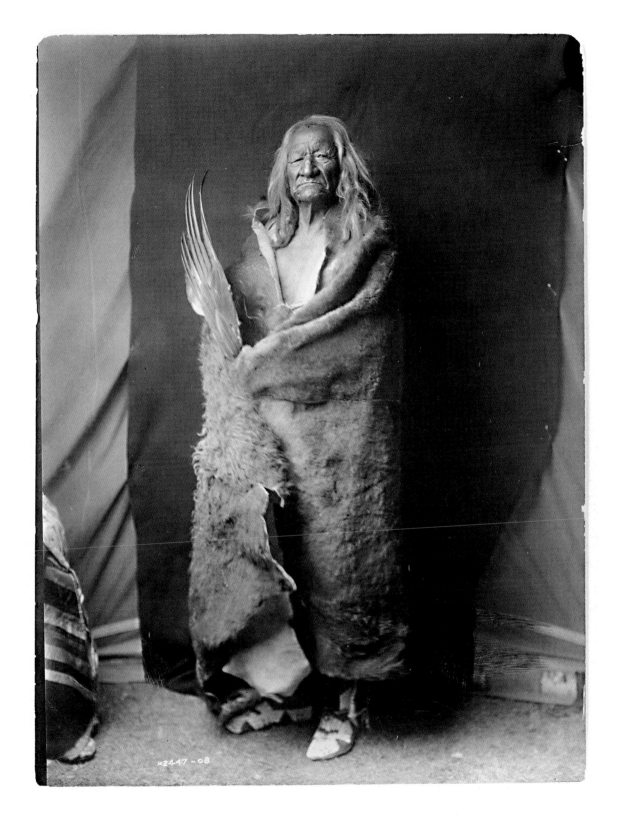

Black Eagle-Assiniboin, ca. 1908

09

LEWIS W. HINE

A father of investigative photojournalism, Lewis W. Hine is best known for his moving portraits of immigrants on Ellis Island, and shocking images of child workers in spinning mills and coal mines.

LEWIS W. HINE

1874 Born in Oshkosh, Wisconsin

1892–1900 After his father's fatal accident, works in various jobs

1901 Attends teaching college, then works as a teacher at the Ethical Culture School, New York

1903 Takes up photography; a series on immigrants on Ellis Island

1906 Freelance work for National Child Labor Committee (NCLC)

1907 Documents cottage labor in New York tenements for the NCLC

1908 Works for the New York State Immigrant Commission

1918 Documents war hospitals in France, Italy and the Balkans

1921–1929 Again active for the NCLC

1931 Records the drought in Kentucky and Arkansas for the Red Cross

1932 *Men at Work*

1940 Dies in Hastings-on-Hudson

"Yes, I want to learn, but can't when I work all the time." These are the words of a 12-year-old who never learned to read, photographed by Hine in 1909 in a cotton mill in Columbia, South Carolina, where the child had already been working for four years. Children labored there as sweepers or back-ropers, repairing torn threads or changing empty spools. Many had no shoes. When inspectors came, the foreman would say, "He just happened in," or "He's helping his sister." In fact the exploitation of child labor was part of the system. Of 40 employees of a mill in Newton, ten were under age. In textile factories in Dallas and Tifton, Hine came across 20 or more child laborers, and dozens in Lancaster—many of them obviously under ten.

Textile manufacturing was not the only field that relied on cheap labor. Hine found child workers in coal mines, canning factories, and glass-blowing companies, and he photographed them as newsboys, shoe shiners, cigar makers, fruit pickers, shrimp shellers. And there were armies of children working morning to night in cottage industries, making doll's dresses, lace, and artificial flowers, or cracking nuts for years on end. Many disadvantaged families, especially immigrants, earned a meager living this way.

Having himself become a factory worker at 18 due to his father's early death—putting in 13-hour days six days a week—Hine spent his life combating child labor, publishing and tirelessly lecturing. An associate then full member of the National Child Labor Committee (NCLC), he published in magazines such as the liberal *Survey*, in newspapers, on posters, and in committee publications that urged Congress to enforce existing laws and improve the protection of children. Hine's "photo stories" were a milestone in the development of photojournalism, which emerged as we now know it only in the 1920s. In 1909 alone, Hine traveled through Georgia, Connecticut, the New England states, Maryland, New Jersey, and North Carolina to visit factories. Sometimes he assumed the identity of a fire protection official or insurance agent in order to gain access. Not seldom was he shown the door.

Towards the end of World War I, Hine went to Europe and photographed war refugees for the American Red Cross and soldiers in French hospitals. He visited ravaged areas in Italy, Greece, and Serbia, then continued his documentation in Belgium and North France. Only a few of these images, movingly attesting to people's will to survive in great need, were published at the time. It was not until the late 1980s that they were finally identified in the Library of Congress, Washington, DC.

Years followed in which, despite professional successes—including the New York Art Directors Club Medal for *The Engineer*—Hine had trouble keeping his head above water, leading him to accept the offer to photograph the construction of the Empire State Building (1930). His pictures of steelworkers balancing at dizzying heights over the city became legendary. Thereafter, Hine resumed his unwearying pursuit of social documentary themes.

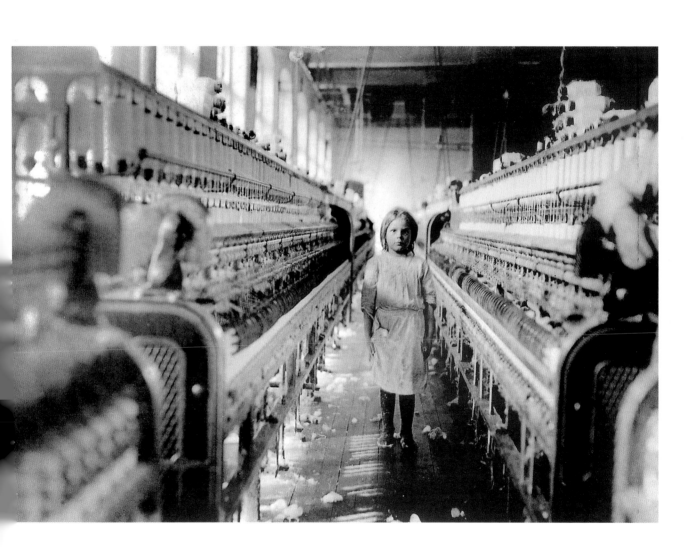

"She just happened in." Newberry, South Carolina, Dec. 1908

10

AUGUST SANDER

August Sander was still very young when he envisaged depicting "people of the 20th century" in a systematic photographic overview arranged by origin and occupation. He devoted years to completing his ambitious work, covering 500 to 600 "types." It became a manifesto to a fidelity to reality, humanism, and tolerance.

AUGUST SANDER

1876 Born in Herdorf (Sieg), Germany

1899–1901 Becomes assistant to an itinerant photographer, traveling through Magdeburg, Halle, Leipzig, Berlin and Dresden

1901 Employed at Atelier Greif, Linz, which he takes over the following year and renames "Sander and Stuckenberg," and of which he is sole proprietor from 1904 onward

1910 Moves to Cologne; begins taking portraits on a regular basis

1927 Exhibition *Menschen des 20. Jahrhunderts* (People of the 20th Century), Kölnischer Kunstverein, Cologne

1929 *Antlitz der Zeit* (The Face of the Times) published, with a foreword by Alfred Döblin

1936 National Socialist Chamber of Art confiscate *Antlitz der Zeit*, the plates being destroyed

1946–1952 Selects photographs for *Köln wie es war* (Cologne as It Once Was)

1964 Dies in Cologne

"The prints in the portfolio were made in the vicinity of my home region, the Westerwald. Due to their closeness to nature, people whose habits I had known from boyhood seemed suitable for realizing my idea of a genealogical portfolio. With this the beginning had been made, and I subordinated all of the types I found to a prototype that possessed all the qualities of the universally human," wrote Sander in 1954. As prototype, he chose the farmer, devoting to this occupation the genealogical portfolio and the first five of more than 45 portfolios. The work as a whole was divided into seven groups: "The Farmer," "The Artisan," "The Women," "The Estates," "The Artists," "The Big City," "The Last Men." Sander's categories in the so-called genealogical portfolio were based on a then-popular doctrine of temperaments, in which people were classified as "earthbound," "philosophical," "impetuous/revolutionary," or "wise." However, he did not pursue this in the portfolios that followed.

Hardly any occupation, profession, or status in life was overlooked. Sander's encyclopedia ranged from confectioner, mason and gardener to industrialist and union member, from Dadaist to wholesale businessman, from mayor to asylum inhabitant, from widower to high school student ... He rarely supplemented the sitters' job description by their name; writers, artists and intellectuals were at first identified only by their initials, and only in the posthumous editions by their full name.

Sander always adapted his concept to changes in society. Thus he included Nazis, individuals persecuted by Nazism, foreign workers, and political prisoners in separate portfolios. One of the prisoners was his own son, Erich, a member of the Socialist Workers' Party of Germany, who was then serving a ten-year sentence (he would die in prison in 1944). "Persecuted Jews" formed a group of their own in *Menschen des 20. Jahrhunderts*. The final portfolio brought together "Idiots, the Sick, Mentally Ill and the Dead," with portraits of, among others, a "Cretin," blind people, midgets, and deceased people on biers. "We must be able to bear seeing the truth," Sander had written about his first exhibition, at the Cologne Art Association, then stated his credo as a photographer: "There is nothing I detest more than sugar-coated photography with its frills, poses and effects." Even the Nazi Chamber of Art got the message, and confiscated *The Face of the Times* and destroyed the printing plates.

Apart from their systematic completeness, Sander's individual portraits have a stringency and penetration that places them among the most significant works in the history of photography. They had a profound influence on many other masters, including Diane Arbus, Robert Häusser, and Richard Avedon. Sander also photographed landscapes, including those along the Rhine, made botanical studies, and created an architectural record of Cologne as it appeared before the war, as well as a documentation of the war-damaged city. Finally, he also carried out commissioned works for architects, artists, and industrial clients.

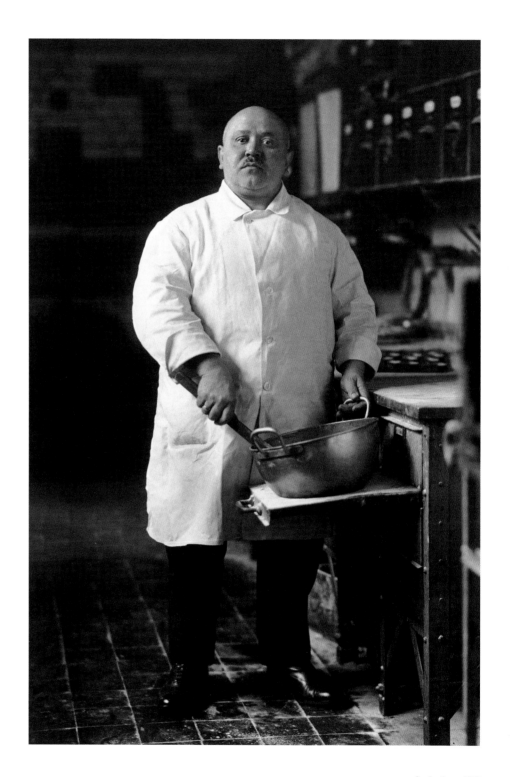

Confectioner, 1928

11

EDWARD STEICHEN

An influential representative of Pictorialism, Edward Steichen was as much at home in war photography as society portraits, fashion and advertising.

EDWARD STEICHEN

Born in Luxembourg and later equally at home in New York and Paris, Steichen for years practiced photography alongside painting, attempting to fuse the two in his turn-of-the-century Pictorialism. Favorite subjects were stretches of forest, whose semi-darkness invoked the mystical realm of Symbolism; portraits of famous artists and poets such as Rodin, Mucha, and Maeterlinck; and female nudes. Like somnambulist nymphs, these figures seemed to spring from the spirit of Gustave Doré. Steichen masterfully contrasted large areas of black with brightly illuminated passages. His 1906 *Storm in the Garden of the Gods*, taken in Colorado, calls up memories of the Swiss artist Arnold Böcklin.

The quarterly *Camera Work*, edited by his friend Alfred Steiglitz from 1903, became a stage for Steichen as for no other photographer: three issues and a supplementary volume were devoted to his work. With great inventiveness, Steichen attempted to expand the painterly potentials of the medium, using such techniques as carbon, platinum and gumbichromate printing, or combinations of these. He also experimented in color photography. Steichen's art photography culminated in his images of Rodin's statue *Balzac*, in which the bronze figure of the poet appears like an epiphany in a dramatically evocative twilight.

The changeover in his work came with the First World War, when in 1917 Steichen suggested to the Air Force that a department of aerial photography be established to clarify details in military maps and record the battlefields and destruction on the Western Front. In the rank of colonel, he provided shocking images of devastated villages and landscapes effaced by bomb craters. The demand for "sharp, clear images" would open his eyes to the unsentimental objectivity that came to the fore in the 1920s. To that point still a successful society portraitist, Steichen abruptly ended his painting career in 1923 by piling up the remaining paintings in his studio and setting fire to them.

Over the next 15 years, Steichen experienced a meteoric rise as head photographer at *Vogue* and *Vanity Fair*. After having produced the first fashion photographs in history worthy of the name, for *Art et Décoration* in 1911, his images now became style-shaping. Innumerable works for the day's leading couturiers and fashion designers followed. When he was advised not to risk his reputation as an art photographer and to publish these pictures anonymously, Steichen made a point of signing them. Nor did he reject lucrative advertising jobs or think himself too good for wallpaper designs or object photographs such as cigarette lighters. Many colleagues looked on such things as a betrayal of the ideals of photography; to him, they represented an expansion of his repertoire. In the meantime, the line outside his portrait studio grew ever longer. The rich, beautiful and famous had themselves portrayed by "America's foremost photographer," avid to "get Steichenized," as the phrase then was. In 1938, Steichen withdrew from commercial photography for good.

He was over 60 when the United States entered the Second World War. With an eye to marshalling domestic support for the war in the Pacific, Steichen was commissioned to mount a propaganda exhibition, *Road to Victory*, shown in 1942 at the Museum of Modern Art, New York.

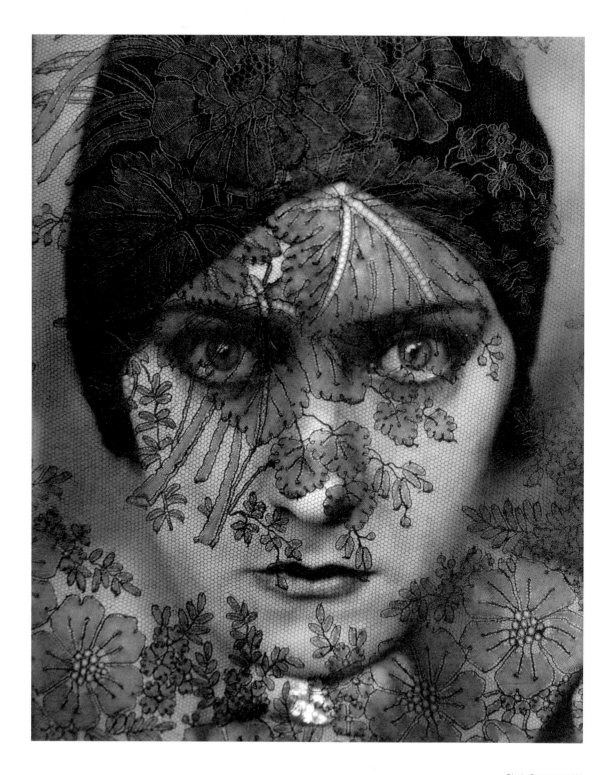

Gloria Swanson, 1928

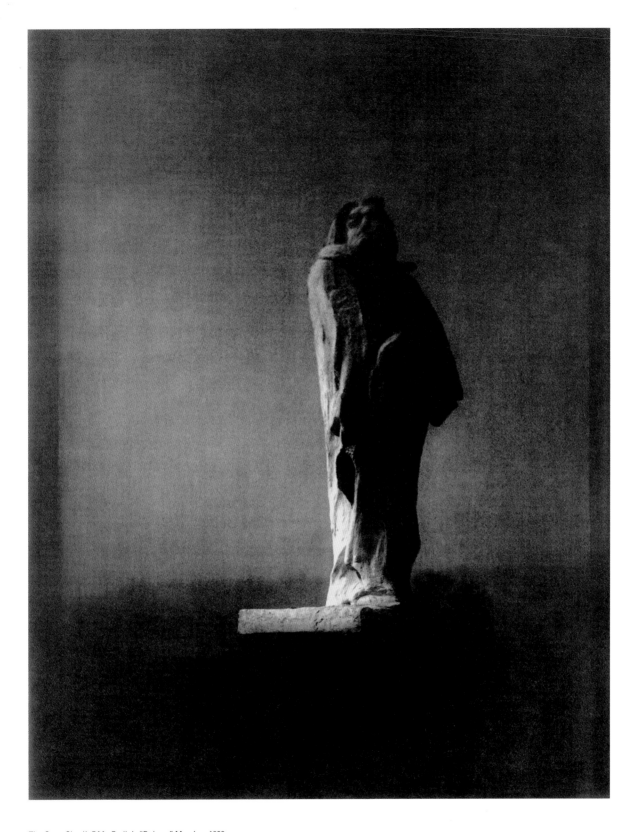

The Open Sky, II: P.M.–Rodin's "Balzac," Meudon, 1908

44

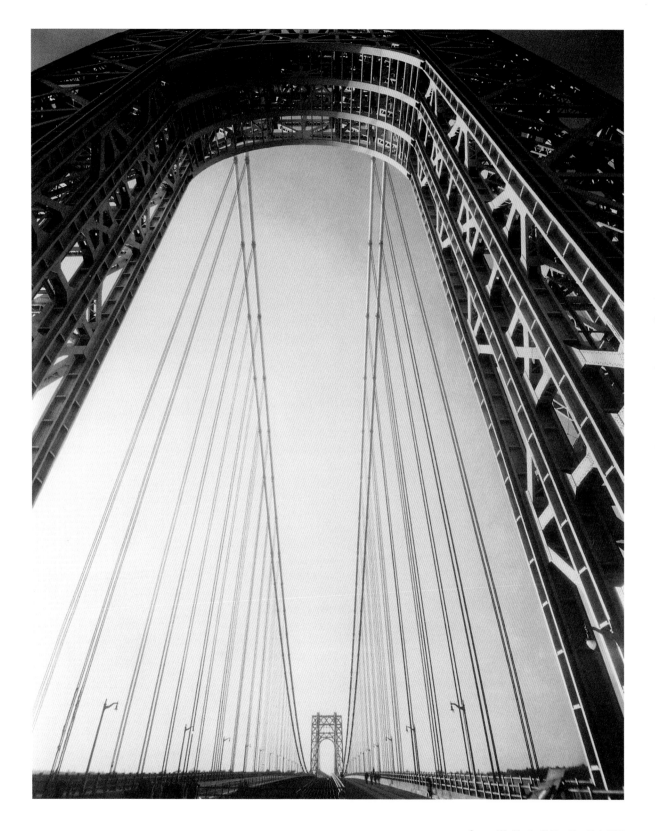

George Washington Bridge, New York, 1931

12

EDWARD WESTON

Edward Weston's search was for absolute form. Far from the madding cry of everyday life, he celebrated the beauties of the American West Coast, the female body, and the plainest of objects.

EDWARD WESTON

Edward Weston's early work was entirely indebted to Pictorialism, with its penchant for profound meanings and a mysterious chiaroscuro or sfumato. A 1920–1921 series devoted to a mansard room with figure, however, revealed a considerable feel for structural clarity and highly sensitive illumination. At the time—as for most of his life—Weston earned a living with studio portraits, especially of children. Straightforward photographs of the seven enormous smokestacks of Armco Steel, an Ohio industrial plant, marked the turning point in Weston's career. The year was 1922. Conversations with Alfred Stieglitz and Paul Strand during the New York trip that followed may have contributed to his decision to take the path of "straight photography" from that point on. The break with everything that had gone before was biographical as well. Weston left his family of five behind in California and spent three years traveling in Mexico with the Italian photographer Tina Modotti. Portraits of his lover ensued, photographs of pyramids, humble houses and squares, objects of folk art, popular murals, and cacti. His objectivity went so far that he lent a palm tree (*Palma Cuernavaca*, 1925) the rigorous look of a factory chimney. Pictures of a washbasin or a toilet bowl (*Excusado*, 1925) had a lapidary beauty of monumental effect. "Here was every sensuous curve of the 'human form divine,'" noted Weston in his daybook, "but minus imperfections."

After his return to California, there emerged his renowned "object-icons," whose majestic lucidity still remains unmatched: a nautilus shell photographed frontally and from various angles, like a chalice; fruit, pumpkins, onions, radishes—but especially peppers, whose sheen prompted him to ever-new variations. A leaf of cabbage was lent the dignity of a Rubens drapery. Feminist commentators have taken offence at the dispassionate care Weston devoted equally to vegetables and his female models. As a reviewer in the *Village Voice* remarked on a New York retrospective years later, "Since he was both a vegetarian and a great lover, he also treated them equally as delicacies."

A bay on the California coast near Big Sur, known as Point Lobos, became as great a treasure trove for the photographer, inspiring images of the beach littered with driftwood and animal cadavers, bones and seaweed, tide pools, and surf-hollowed rocks. For Weston, this was a laboratory for the generation of a new, sculptural cosmos.

Two Guggenheim fellowships, in 1937 and 1939, freed Weston from commercial jobs. He traveled through California, Arizona, New Mexico, Oregon and Washington, concentrating on landscapes. One quarter of his superb life's work emerged during these two years alone. From beetles' tracks in the sand to monumental panoramas, Weston captured the entire range of landscape features and events. Many of the views and texture studies were so strongly abstracted as to anticipate the painting of Abstract Expressionism, notably those of Jackson Pollock, Mark Tobey, and Willem de Kooning.

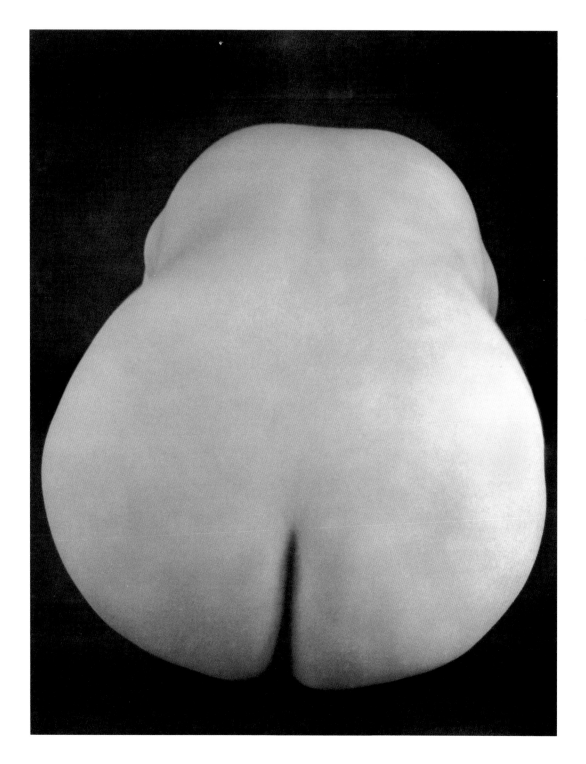

Nude, 1926

13 MAN RAY

Man Ray was a tireless experimenter. His most important works were done in a visual twilight zone, in a tense interplay between painting, sculpture, and photography.

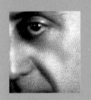

Man Ray was no conventional photographer who combed the city and countryside in search of motifs. His world was the studio, and especially the darkroom, where he coaxed visions from photographic paper with silver and salt, like an alchemist. A Surrealist and friend of Marcel Duchamp, he probably thought it too banal to simply portray his artist friends. Ray sought unconventional poses and arrangements, alienated his subjects by means of surprising accessories, extreme cropping, or "solarization." As his working prints reveal, the definitive—frequently extreme—croppings were often established in a second step. Some of his models appeared on the verge of sleep (*Dora Maar*, 1936), others emerging from nocturnal darkness (*Salvador Dalí*, 1929), still others flipped from positive to negative (*André Breton*, ca. 1930). He pasted glass beads on the cheeks of a girl, Lydia, to show her "crying" in the famous photograph *Tears* (1932), an artificiality derived by the director Man Ray from the props of the film world.

Man Ray was a specialist in the field of the female nude. The list of illustrious befriended beauties he photographed unclad was a long one: Meret Oppenheim, Lee Miller, Nusch Eluard, Suzy Solidor, and his favorite model, the legendary Kiki de Montparnasse, queen of the bohemian world of Paris. Nor did he shy away from objects of a fetishistic character, portraying Mlle. Dorita in the coils of a python (1930), or Lee Miller with anatomical weaves of wire placed around her head or arm (1930). This was the Art Deco period, intrigued by the theme of man and machine.

His series of female faces, stylized and made-up to the verge of the mask-like, culminated in an unusual composition. Next to the head of Kiki, resting with eyes closed, he placed an African Baule mask (Ivory Coast), creating a highly evocative Surrealist icon (*Noire et Blanche*, 1926). The power of this image was surpassed only by *Le Violon d'Ingres* (1924), the back view of a nude wearing a turban, Dadaistically alienated by the addition of the two "clefs" of a cello. Man Ray's sense of the puzzle of human perception was so strong that even his photographs for the fashion magazine *Harper's Bazaar* showed that he was not taken in by beautiful illusion.

In his Rayograms, made without a camera, Man Ray's visual fantasies came to full flower. Placing various objects directly on photographic paper under the enlarger and exposing them, he fixed the shadows they cast. Feathers, coils of string, springs, and other unorthodox objects formed semi-abstract compositions in white on black. The process enriched the repertoire of Surrealist techniques by a new and enthusiastically received variant.

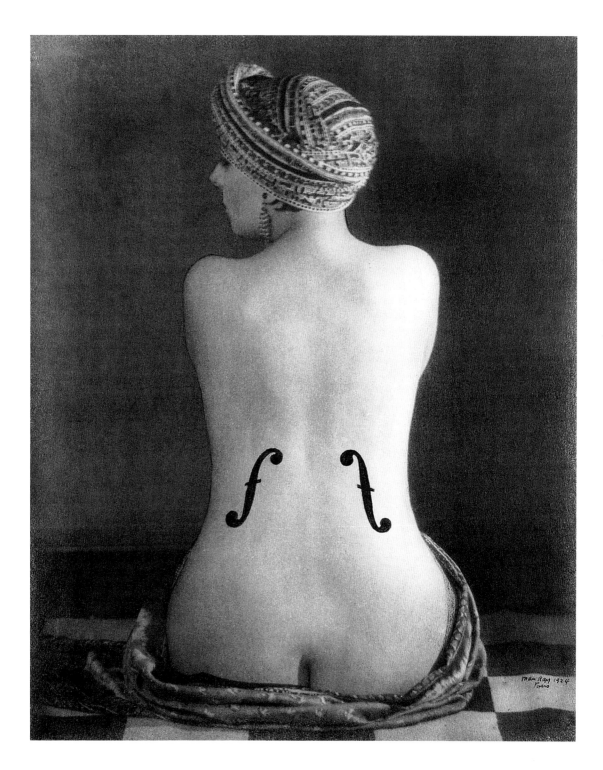

Violon d'Ingres, 1924

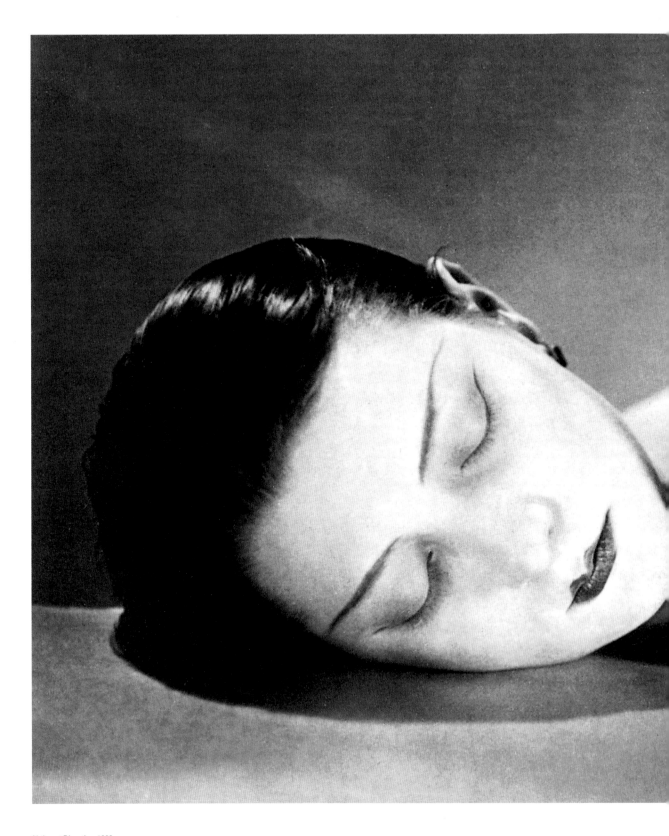

Noire et Blanche, 1926

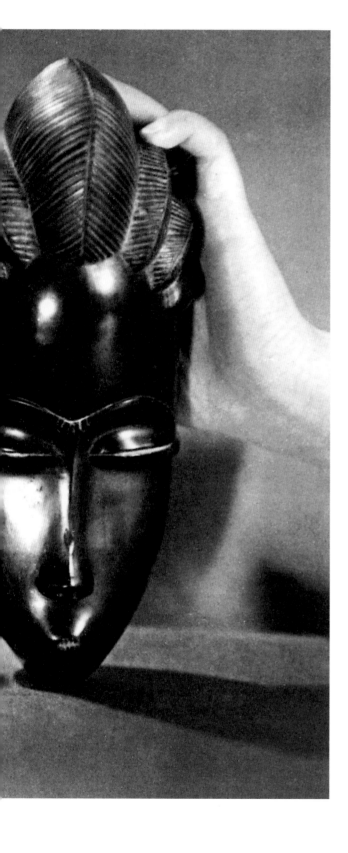

14 PAUL STRAND

The photos Paul Strand published in the final (1917) issue of *Camera Work* were a bombshell. As the reveries of Pictorialism faded, Strand supplanted its tranquillizing soft-focus with a bracing stimulant—Verism.

The years 1915–1916 brought a change in Paul Strand's work. Still lifes with fruit, passersby in New York parks, and steamers emitting picturesque plumes of smoke, suddenly made way for the turned rungs of a chair back, porcelain bowls, and the shadows cast by a balcony balustrade forming dramatically plunging lines. Strand replied to Stieglitz's studies of clouds over Lake George by showing a section of house roof against the cloudy sky over the Twin Lakes in Connecticut at such an oblique angle that it seemed caught in an earthquake. Sergei Eisenstein or Alexander Rodchenko would have enjoyed these "Constructivist" experiments, done at a time when the terms to describe them had yet to be invented.

The name Paul Strand stands for an objective, documentary style that extends both to figures and landscapes, objects and events. After his hoped-for breakthrough as a film director came to nothing and he moved to the French provinces, Strand devoted himself in 1950–1952 to a book—*La France de profil*—in which the face of rural France was recorded in an unusually objective way. Avoiding touristic clichés, Strand focused on normal, everyday village life. He photographed the doors of humble houses, geraniums on window sills, the façades of bistros. Portrait after portrait of the inhabitants emerged, from artisans to elderly people resting on benches. The village world was framed by gently rolling hills under a spacious sky. Crosses and gravestones evoked the natural cycle of life.

Even on his earlier trips to the American Southwest, in 1926 and following years, Strand had shown less interest in the monumental scenery than in the ordinary beauties of the towns. He exploited the play of light and shade to produce images of great intensity. Bare house walls shorn of decoration and crumbling façades seemed impregnated with the life of these places, past and present. The back of the white stucco church of San Francisco de Assisi, in Ranchos de Taos, New Mexico, appeared in many photographs of 1930 and the two following years. The "pure form" of this cubic ensemble intrigued many artists. Yet indicatively, instead of making a modernistic form of the building, as he had in his earlier work, Strand now let it speak with its own voice. During the 1930s he also undertook international assignments, visiting Spain and China.

Strand continued to travel widely during the 1950s, visiting, among other places, Egypt, Romania, Hungary, and Ghana; his images of his trip to the island of Uist in the Outer Hebrides in 1953 were published in 1962 as *Tir a'Mhurain*, while his photographs of Italy, especially of the small town of Luzzara in Reggio Emilia, appeared in *Un paese*, 1955.

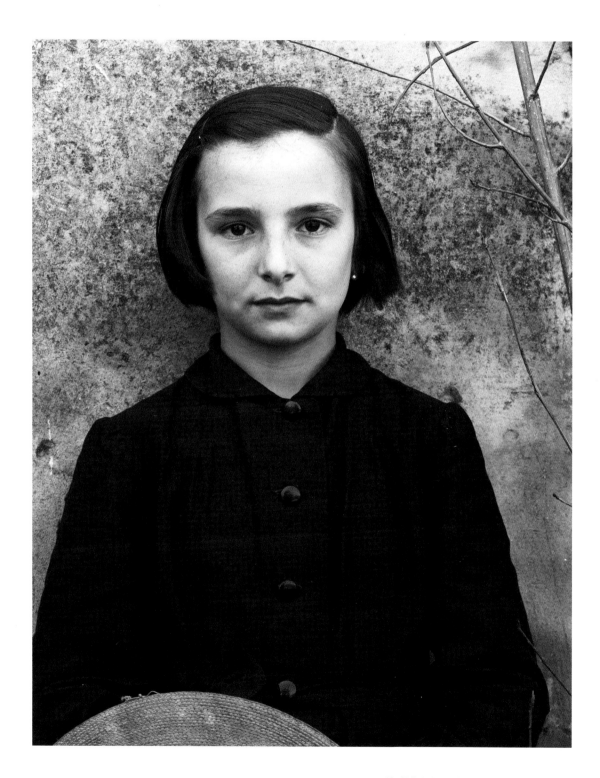

The Tailor's Apprentice, Luzzara, Italy (variant), 1953

ALEXANDER RODCHENKO

Alexander Rodchenko championed the new aesthetic that was propagated in the wake of the Russian Revolution. He painted, made photo-collages, and created Constructivist sculptures suspended from the ceiling. The vertiginous perspectives of his photographs became symbols of the intoxication with the future that pervaded Bolshevist Russia.

ALEXANDER RODCHENKO

In the years following the overthrow of Czarist rule, the young USSR rapidly recapitulated the cultural innovations that had been denied to the country for centuries. Never did the future seem more promising than in 1920s Moscow. Every field of art became a laboratory, devoted to a modernization of perception and a "New Vision." As a sculptor, Alexander Rodchenko had already turned the world upside down in his suspended *Constructions in Space*, and when he bought a camera in 1924, his photographs proved no less revolutionary.

His first extensive cycle, *Views of a Building on Myasnicka Street*, 1925, show a ten-story brick building in precipitous perspective from below, with iron-railed balconies stacked tightly over one another. In other views, the fire escape shoots up nearly vertically—a daring anticipation of Laszlo Moholy-Nagy's *Balconies of the Bauhaus in Dessau*, 1927. In his images of courtyards and squares, Rodchenko likewise abandoned the "normal" point of view, picturing people and things obliquely from above, and employing cast shadows as compositional means. "Especially from above looking downwards and from below looking upwards—these are the most interesting vantage points for contemporary photography," he stated in 1928.

The forced industrialization of agrarian Russia entailed a great social and aesthetic challenge for the avant-garde. Rodchenko first tested the new field of photo-reportage in 1928, in a series on the daily *Pravda* that recorded the paper's production from typesetting and layout to printing. For the journal *DAES*, in 1929, he documented manufacturing at the AMO automobile plant, proving a master of the "gripping detail," as he himself put it. For his 1930 record of a mass scene like *Dynamo–Moscow*, Rodchenko likewise found a new visual idiom.

His photo series on the Pioneers, including *Pioneer with Horn*, 1930, the boy's face pictured from below in daring foreshortening, became icons of the new cultural upheaval in the USSR. *Dive into the Water*, a brilliant photographic experiment, showed a high diver rolled almost into the shape of a ball in the upper right corner of the picture. With images of his mother and the poet and publicist Vladimir Mayakovsky (both 1924), Rodchenko produced master portraits of the new era. Under Stalin, the burgeoning cultural and political orthodoxy harassed the artist with charges of formalism. Rodchenko abandoned photography in 1942.

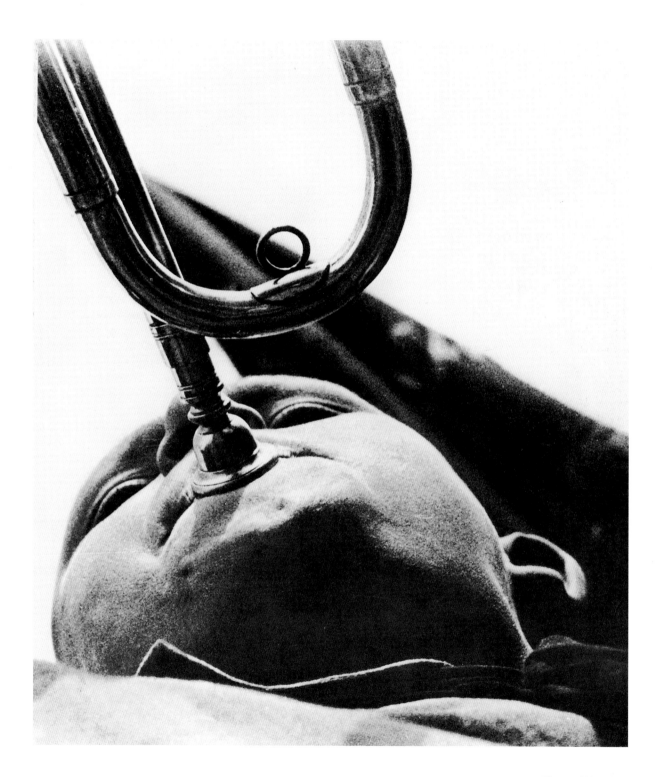

Pioneer with Horn, 1930

16 ANDRÉ KERTÉSZ

Perhaps it was André Kertész's self-evaluation as an amateur, a perpetual beginner who continually rediscovers the world anew, that ensured the vitality and originality of his work over seven decades.

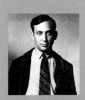

ANDRÉ KERTÉSZ

André Kertész was a master of form and plane, the laws of volume and space. His photographs of city squares and streets from a high vantage point lent order to the bustle of life. New York's Washington Square became an especially fruitful site for Kertész: footprints and tire tracks in the snow, tree branches, fences, benches, and milling passersby provided the elements from which he composed visual chamber music. Rather than practicing street photography as a form of close-up sociology, he produced finely equilibrated urban views. This tendency had already marked his early work in Hungary, even though his holiday scenes, images of gypsies and itinerant musicians, village communities, friends, and moments in the trenches of the First World War amounted to an eloquent record of the final days of the Austro-Hungarian Empire. *The Underwater Swimmer*, taken in 1917 in Esztergom, was Kertész's most famous early work.

In his French period (1925–1936), apart from portraits, direct views of the human face became rarer. Kertész focused his lens on the structure of the city, finding comprehensive spatial harmonies in which people tend to figure as accessories. Unlike Brassaï's, his images of Paris by night had no air of vice about them. Where the former sensed low instincts, Kertész found plays of light and shadow.

On visits to painters and sculptors, he portrayed not only them but also their studios, in still lifes of utensils. *Mondrian's Studio* (1926) is a light-flooded interior reminiscent of a Cubist collage by Picasso; *Mondrian's Glasses and Pipe*, of the same year, a still life composed in the style of the New Vision, whose compositional clarity is surpassed only by the famous *Fork* (1928), an advertising photograph for the Bruckmann Company, of Heilbronn, Germany.

Perhaps intentionally spoofing the idea of valid form, for the humor magazine *Le Sourire* Kertész posed nude models in front of a distorting mirror (1933) that stretched and compressed their limbs into novel sculptural configurations. People, faces and objects were subjected to the same treatment.

Finally, the skyscraper city enriched the works of Kertész's American period (1936–1962) with new motifs. Yet the poetic spirit that marked the Hungarian's art throughout his career, objective in a rather un-French way, continued to inform these late images.

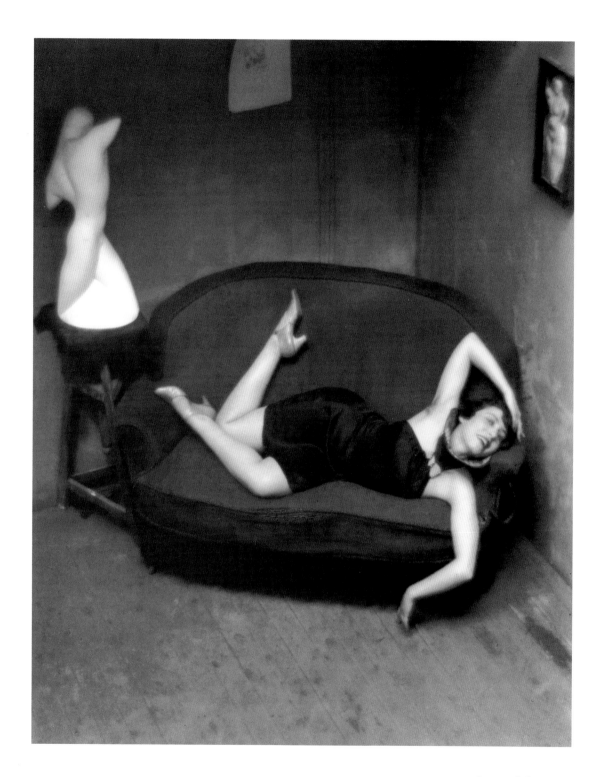

Danseuse Burlesque, 1926

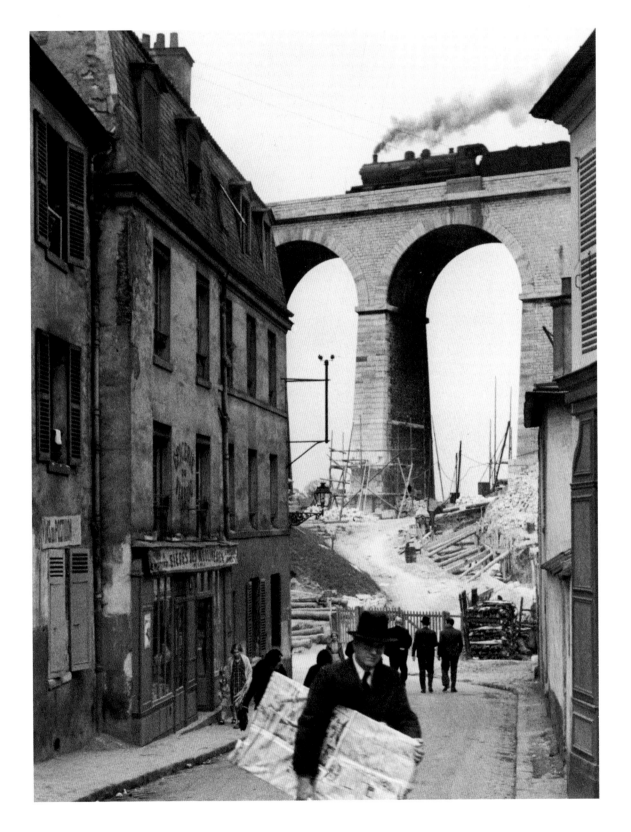

Meudon, 1928

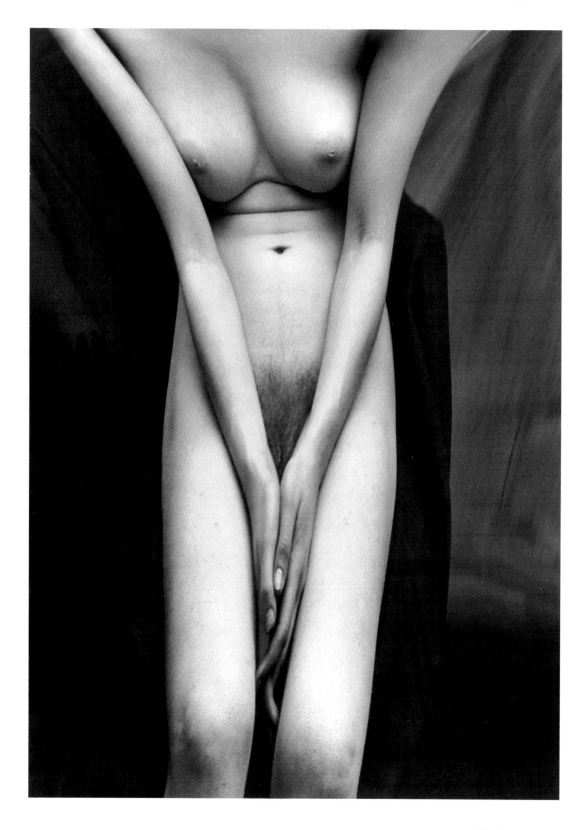

Distortion no. 168, 1933

17

JACQUES-HENRI LARTIGUE

The privileged life of Jacques-Henri Lartigue, spent between Cannes, Nice, Deauville and Paris, was like a serialized novel in the glossies. His elegant images capture both the charmed life of the wealthy and his own fascination with the age of speed.

JACQUES-HENRI LARTIGUE

1894 Born in Courbevoie, France

1900 Takes his first photographs, with a camera owned by his father, who in the coming years will present him with the latest models

1911 Photographs automobile races in Monaco

1915 Attends the Académie Julian, Paris

1920–1921 Takes first autochromes, in the park of La Garoupe palace, Cap d'Antibes

1922 Exhibits his paintings at the Galerie Georges-Petit, Paris

1923 Takes his earliest photographs with flash

1925 Takes photographs of the Promenade des Anglais, Nice, in a heavy storm

1932 Contributes to the filming of *Les Aventures du roi Pausole*

1963 Retrospective at MoMA, New York

1970 Publishes *Instants de ma vie* (Diary of a Century)

1986 Dies in Nice

Jacques-Henri Lartigue was a wunderkind of photography. At ten, he snapped his cousin, Simone, with her dog on the beach of Villerville, and his brother, Maurice (Zissou), jumping off a boat. By the time he was a teenager he had already filled an album with snapshots worthy of a master. People jumping, hopping, suspended in midair, falling—the young photographer loved such motifs. And because movement intrigued him most, he always had a camera at hand when cycling, swimming, at soapbox derbies, auto races, and flying contests. The photographs of Zissou and his exuberant cousins were merely the point of departure for a vibrant photographic career. It was the spontaneous gaze of the child that saved Lartigue from emulating the melancholy mood of the art photography of the day.

His oeuvre is reminiscent of the private album of a privileged family, later supplemented by a circle of prominent friends. What diversions they enjoyed, from airfield to beach, outings on the yacht or in the Hispano-Suiza, at tennis, the horse races, skiing or skating in Chamonix. Astonishing, how many months of his life Lartigue spent in luxury hotels—the Negresco, in Nice, being only one of many. To him the good life, so temptingly illustrated in *Vogue* or *Harper's Bazaar*, was simply his birthright, and he lived it among film stars, artists, and countesses. An ambitious painter throughout his life, Lartigue discovered moments of very personal grace beyond the galas and premieres of this *dolce vita*. He captured the fleeting joys of life under the Mediterranean sun like no other. And perhaps this is the real secret behind his art: Lartigue's images are full of *esprit*, that irony-spiced, so quintessentially French attitude to life.

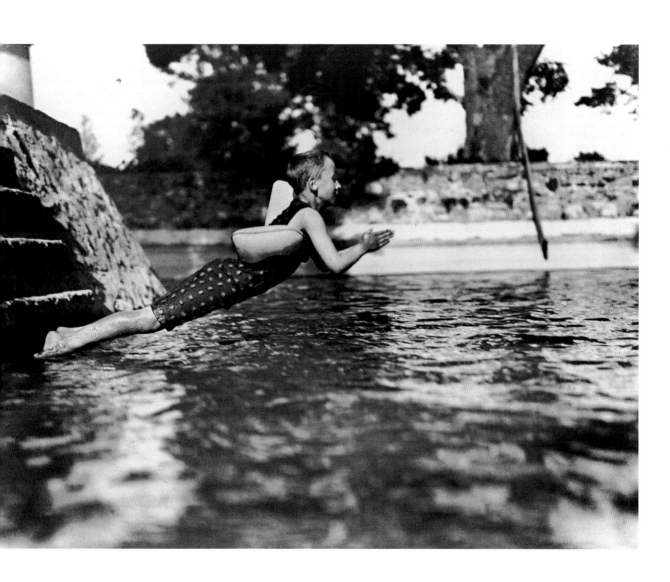

Dédé Rouzat, 1911

18

DOROTHEA LANGE

Dorothea Lange's stark photos acted as the conscience of her age. One of her images from the Great Depression, *Migrant Mother* (1936), became so famous it obscured the remainder of her rich and diverse oeuvre.

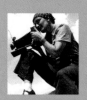

DOROTHEA LANGE

The misery that followed in the wake of the 1929 New York stock-market crash was devastating, costing millions their jobs and homes, forcing them to go on the road in search of work. Dorothea Lange's photographs show lines of people waiting for welfare payments, people sleeping in the streets, people looking for a job, moving from town to town. Others had long since been forced to exchange their apartment for a car, a tent, or a hovel. Lange visited workers' camps at the edge of cotton and tobacco fields and orchards, the city slums, San Francisco's soup kitchens (*White Angel Breadline*, 1933), and the demonstrations and general strike that took place there in 1934. On commission from Roy Striker of the Resettlement Administration (RA, later FSA), Lange sought out areas worst hit by the Depression, to record the fate of the stranded and destitute. From fall 1935 to fall 1936 alone, she covered 1,700 miles through 14 states. She photographed families with undernourished children in ragged clothes, once-proud workers and farmers at the end of their endurance. The terrible drought that hit the Oklahoma Dust Bowl in 1936 forced even sharecroppers to abandon their fields. And yet, even in the face of such strokes of fate, Lange firmly believed these people retained their pride, resolution, and courage.

In 1942, citizens of Japanese origin were confined in internment camps built expressly for the purpose. Lange recorded these, as well as the harvest workers who streamed in from Mexico to offset the dearth of farm labor caused by the war. A portrait photographer from the start, Lange devoted herself to street photography only marginally. She looked for the traces of human experiences and feelings in people's faces, the expression in their eyes, their gestures. And her pictures teach us what confrontation with reality means. A statement by the Elizabethan writer Francis Bacon was pinned to her darkroom door: "The contemplation of things as they are, without error or confusion, without substitution or imposture, is in itself a nobler thing than a whole harvest of invention."

There were three rules to which Lange always adhered: "Whatever I photograph, I do not molest or tamper with or arrange. Second: a sense of place. Whatever I photograph, I try to picture as part of its surroundings, as having roots. Third: a sense of time. Whatever I photograph, I try to show as having its position in the past or in the present."

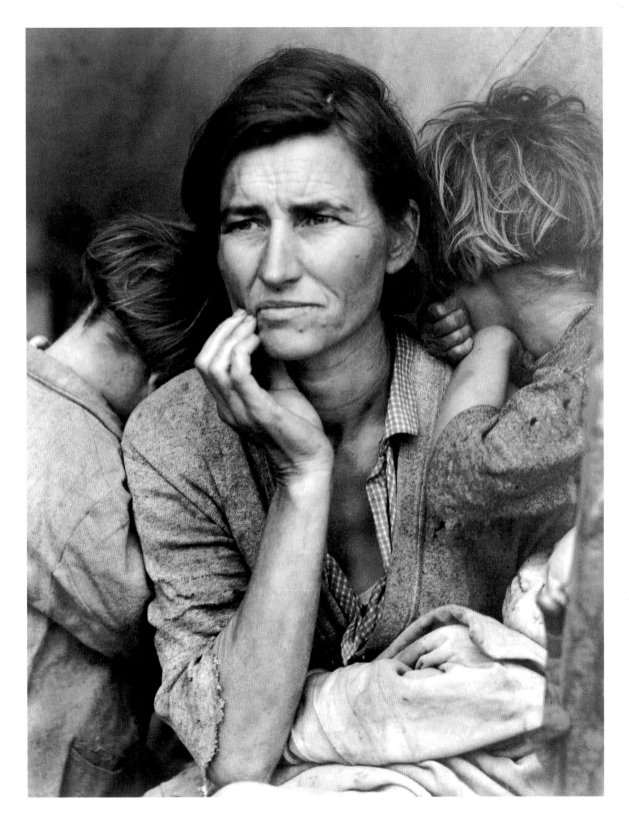

Migrant Mother, Nipomo, California, March 1936

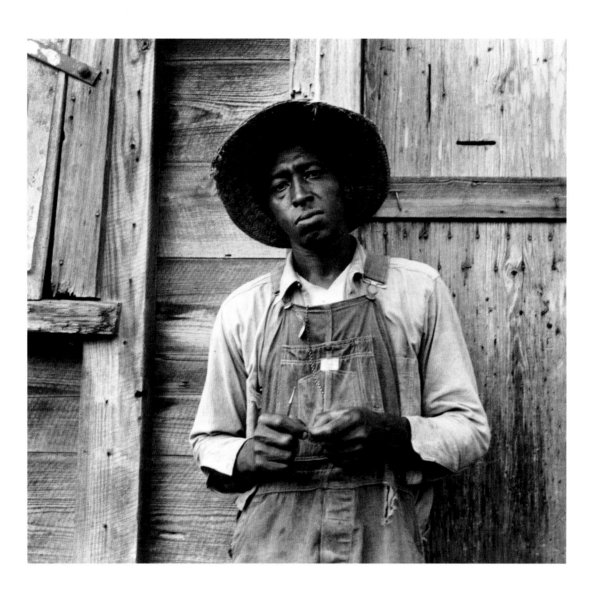

Sharcropper, Chatham County, North Carolina, July 1939

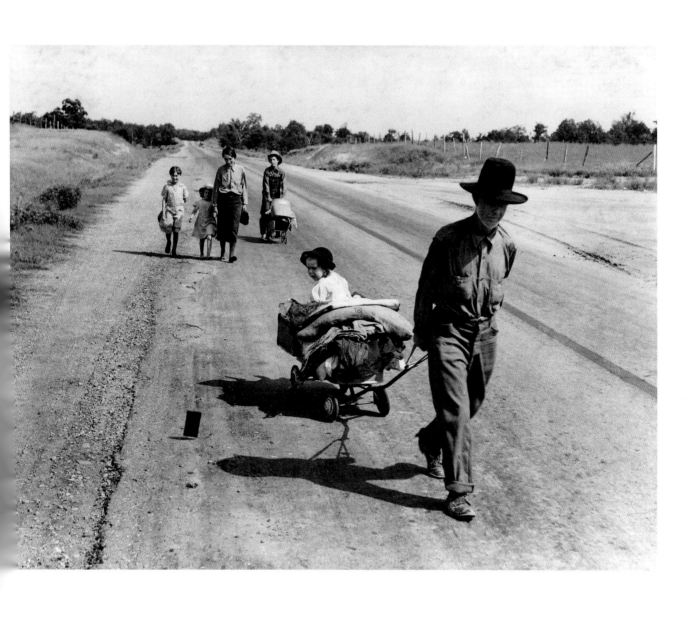

Homeless Family, Oklahoma, June 1938

19

JOSEF SUDEK

Josef Sudek, who spent his entire life in one city, Prague, became one of photography's greatest poets. Working in the isolation of his studio and local gardens, he developed a hermetic world of simple things—and light.

JOSEF SUDEK

1896 Born in Kolín, Bohemia (today Czech Republic)

1908–1910 Attends the Royal Technical Trade School, Kutná Hora; begins taking photographs

1910–1913 Serves an apprenticeship in book binding

1916 Loses his right arm in the war

1922–1924 Attends the State School of Graphic Arts, Prague

1922 Co-founds the Prague Photographic Club (expelled in 1924)

1924 Co-founds the Czech Photographic Society

1927 Establishes a studio for portrait and advertising photography

1930s Runs the Sudek Gallery of Visual Art

1976 Dies in Prague

If we looked at Josef Sudek's early images without knowing his dates, we might be excused for thinking him a turn-of-the-century Pictorialist. So important was atmosphere to him that the pictures he took in 1922–1927 for *Invalid War Veterans' Home* recall scenes from a cozy inn. Objective social reportage was not Sudek's aim. Yet over the following years he would find a link with certain tendencies of the period. The complex geometries in some of the images taken in St. Veit's Cathedral in Prague (1924–1928) recalled the spirit of Russian Constructivism. The straightforward object, advertising, and architectural photographs he began in 1927 to supply to an aesthetically advanced clientele were very much along the lines of the Bauhaus and the "New Vision."

Apart from his commercial activities, Sudek produced highly sophisticated series: *Window in my Studio* (1940–1959), *Vanished Statues* (1952), *In the Enchanted Garden* (1954–1959), *Glass Labyrinths* (1968–1972), *Labyrinths* (1972–1975). These were supplemented by numbers of still lifes, composed of various seashells, eggs, simple drinking glasses, bread, an unexposed roll of film, even a sponge and head of cabbage. Into these images entered the poetry for which his daily business left him no time. A sculptor in light, a true "light-painter," for over 14 years Sudek recorded the changing light at his studio window: dotted with raindrops, steamed with humidity, frosted over—by day, in twilight, by night. "He wrestled with light like Jacob with the angel," as the poet Jaroslav Seifert recalled. Cellophane and oiled paper with a seashell placed on it could form the point of departure for a drama in light on which he worked for hours on end.

In parallel, photographs of Prague gardens and parks, and of landscapes in the city's environs emerged (the latter taken from about 1947, with a panorama camera). Many of these images showed a return of the numinous mood of Pictorialism, mentioned above. In several works taken in the garden of his architect friend Otto Rothmayer, Sudek rang changes on the theme of the *Enchanted Garden*. Modern white garden furniture, occasionally supplemented by sculpture fragments or stone balls, figured as accessories to a locale spirited into a state of mystery. Touches of surrealism alternated with lyrical moods.

As the piles of crumpled paper he later captured in his *Labyrinth* series indicate, up to a year before his death Sudek not only remained on a search for a bygone era but reacted to the aesthetic ferment of the present day.

The first monograph (with 232 intaglio plates) was published in 1956.

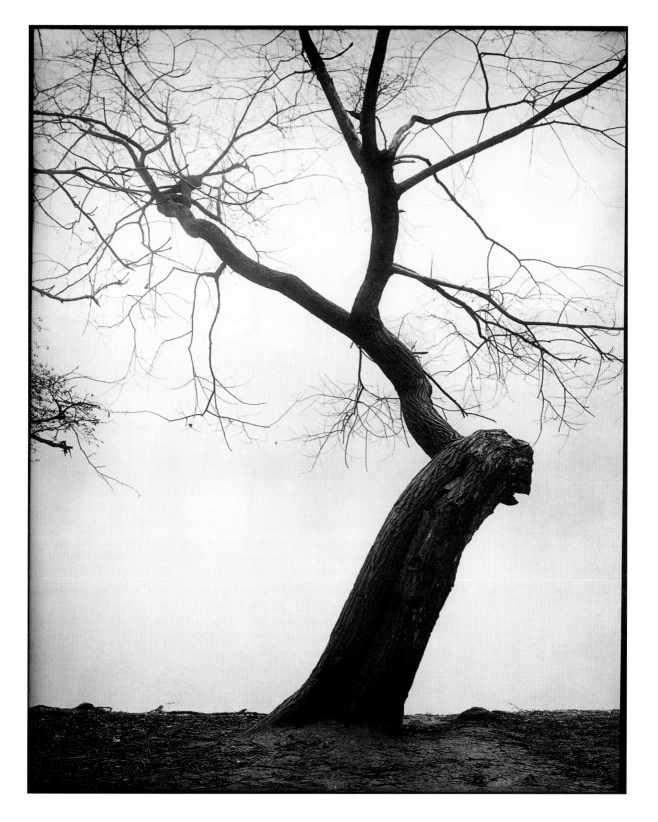

Walk on the Schützeninsel, 1946–1966

20

ALBERT RENGER-PATZSCH

Renger-Patzsch created a pictorial universe that encompasses technology, architecture, landscape, and nature in equal measure. He was as devoted to the microcosm of plants and crystals as to the giant industrial plants of the Ruhrgebiet.

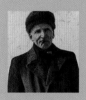

ALBERT RENGER-PATZSCH

1897 Born in Würzburg, Germany

1909 Begins to take photographs

1916–1918 Serves in the army

1919–1921 Studies chemistry at Dresden Technical College

1921–1924 Works as head of photo archive; *Die Welt der Pflanze* (The World of Plants)

1925 First solo exhibition

1928 *Die Welt ist schön* (The World is Beautiful)

1929–1932 Documents the cityscapes and industry in the Ruhrgebiet

1933 Teaches at the Folkwangschule, Essen

1933–1945 Wins commissions from industry, publishers, and architects

1966 Dies in Wamel, Germany

Others would have gone farther afield, but even the dingy tenements and suburban streets on the city periphery caught the eye of Albert Renger-Patzsch. A diverse agglomeration of poster pillar, power line and factory chimney next to the firewall of a building could inspire him to an image—a celebration of austerity. He was even satisfied with a sagging fence outside an isolated house in the Froschlake Development in Dortmund-Marten. Almost all of these pictures were uninhabited, yet they told an eloquent story about the difficult lives of the people who lived under such conditions.

Drama was far from Renger-Patzsch's mind. His Ruhr Valley landscapes were not heroic panoramas of the kind Edward Weston found in California and New Mexico. Waste heaps, a sandpit, or a garden colony near Essen, with a row of smoke-belching factory stacks along the upper margin (1929), sufficed him for a composition. He also sought out "intact" landscapes, devoting photography books to the North Sea Halligen Islands, the Ore Mountains, Lake Möhnsee, and the Rheingau region—and especially to forests and even individual trees.

Admittedly the drama of a factory chimney taken from a very low vantage point interested him (*Kauper, Viewed from Below*, 1928), but Renger-Patzsch made no dogma of Constructivism (in the manner of Alexander Rodchenko), preferring to capture industrial plants from a detached middle distance. The images of the two Essen mines Bonifacius (1940–1941) and Katharina (1956) were compelling compositions of cubic masses, framed in daring excerpts. His photographs of pitheads, heaters, Bessemer converters, and trestle bridges were pioneering achievements in the field of modern industrial archaeology.

Renger-Patzsch lent his manufacturing and advertising photographs an intensity far beyond the norm for commercial photography. Jobs for Kaffee Hag, Ruhrglas and Schott inspired him to aesthetically ambitious still lifes. "The charms of photography," in his eyes, lay "in halftones, the division of the plane, and the course of lines." Photographs like *Pressing Iron for Shoe Manufacturing* and *Shoe Lasts at the Fagus Works, Alfeld*, both 1926, became icons of the genre, worthy of being placed alongside Weston's *Peppers* (1930). The retorts for the Schott Glassworks in Jena (1934) possess a virtually celestial transparency. The scaly skin of an adder, the spines of a cactus, not to mention blossoms and plants (*Agave americana*, 1923), reflected the same dedication to detail. If he had had his own way, Renger-Patzsch would have entitled his 1928 book, *Die Welt ist schön* (The World is Beautiful), introduced by 20 botanical photographs, simply *Things*.

In 1943 he photographed the Western Wall fortifications in Normandy and Brittany; the following year a large part of his archive was destroyed during the bombardment of Essen.

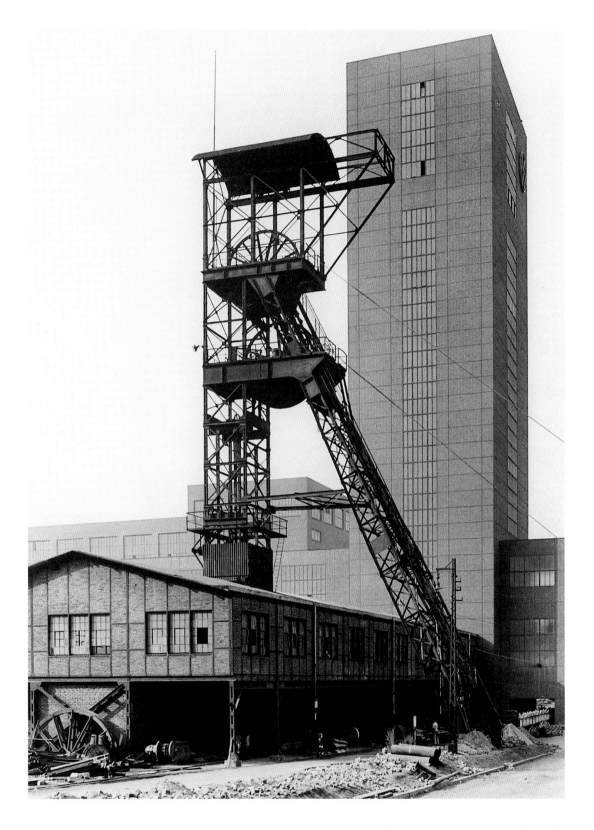

"Katharina" Colliery in Essen, "Ernst Tengelmann" Shaft, 1956

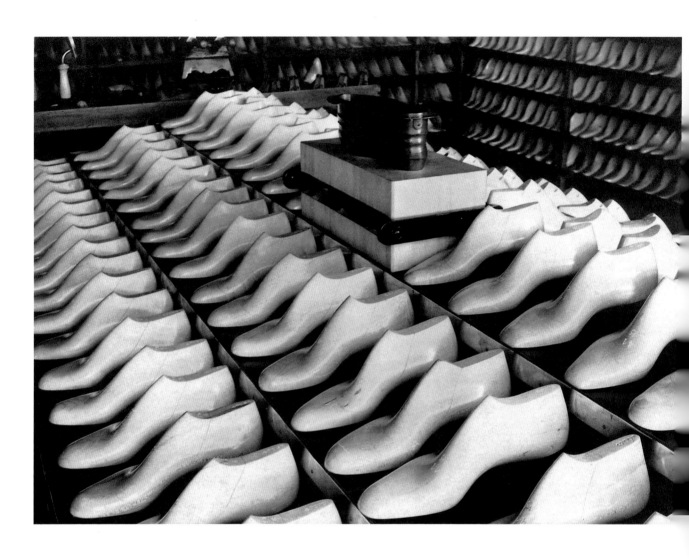

Shoe Lasts at the Fagus Factory, Alfeld, 1926

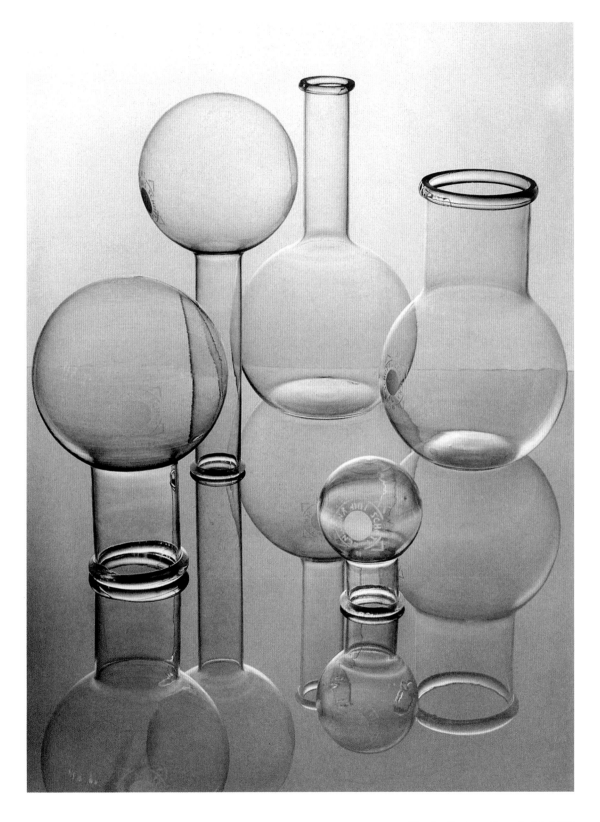

Glass Tumbler, Jenaer Glaswerke Schott, 1934

21

BRASSAÏ

Brassaï was fascinated by the overlooked—the grafitti on the walls of Paris buildings, the "unintentional sculptures" of crumpled tickets and toothpaste. But it is as a recorder Paris night-life that he is best remembered.

He woke at sunset and did not return home until sunrise—this was the nocturnal life Brassaï led after his arrival in Paris. His first book, *Paris by Night*, collected the most picturesque images from his nightly jaunts: buildings looming over empty streets from whose depths the gaslight filtered magically skywards, the ghostly quais along the Seine, the deserted station of Saint-Lazare. Cascades of light over the fountain on the Place de la Concorde were confronted with a warming fire built under a bridge by homeless men. Paris by night—stray cats, patrolling gendarmes, tired prostitutes, workers tarring a street. It would be over 40 years before Brassaï entrusted his most challenging images to a publisher: the "secret Paris" of prostitutes and bordellos, the gay and lesbian clubs, the "Negro balls," backstage at the Follies-Bergère...

In 1932 Brassaï began to record the scrawls and scratchings on the walls of Paris buildings, and in 1934 published them in the Surrealist journal *Minotaure*—a "language of the walls" that was more than mere childish pranks. In addition to figures and heads that recalled cave paintings and prehistoric rock drawings, in addition to masks, faces and animals, he discovered configurations he would later collect under the titles "La Magie" and "Images primitives." "These terse symbols," wrote Brassaï in *Minotaure*, "are nothing less than the beginnings of language; these monsters, these demons, these heroes, these phallic gods are nothing less than elements of a mythology." In 1950 Brassaï became virtually an archaeologist of this unofficial art when he began noting the locations of the images in a sketchbook, "in order to revisit them later under better lighting conditions, or to find them again many years later and record their changes." It was this appreciation for marginal art that prompted John Szarkowski to contrast the "angel of darkness" Brassaï to the blithe spirit of Cartier-Bresson, saying that Brassaï's sensibility, his pleasure in the primitive, fantastic, ambivalent, even bizarre, originated from an earlier age.

To Brassaï we owe the first documentation of Picasso's work in sculpture, including many fragile creations in paper that have since been lost or destroyed, as well as a record of the conversations he had with the artist. And he was an avid visitor of the studios of his illustrious artist friends, whose personalities he recorded for posterity.

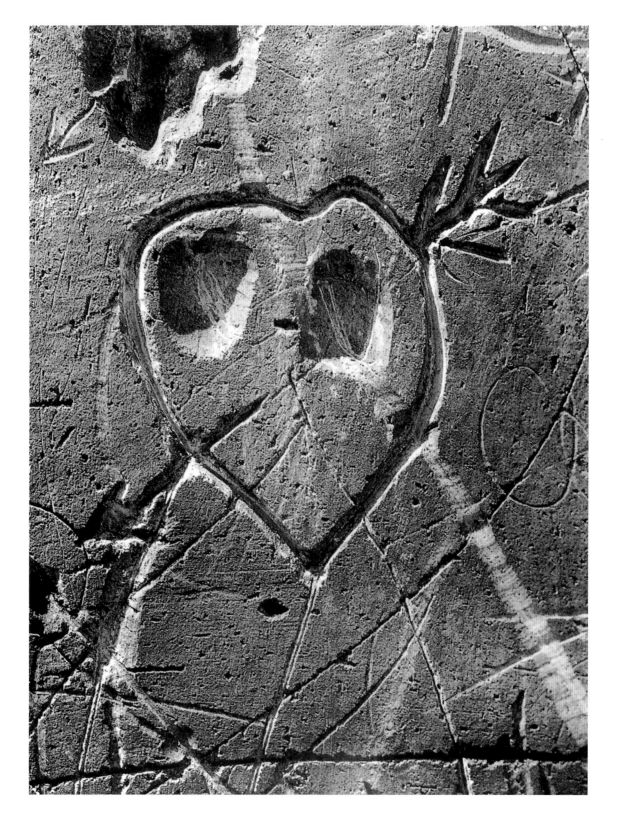

Love (undated)

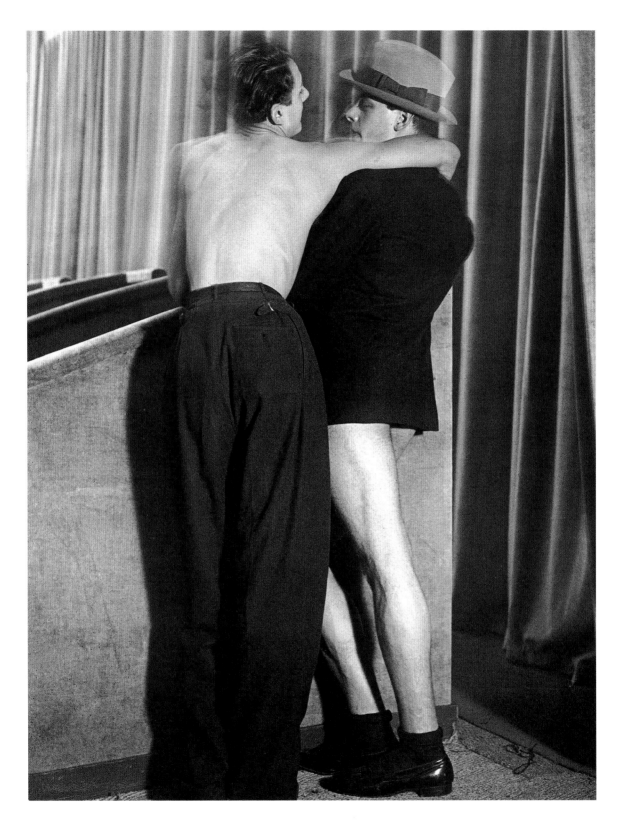

A Suit for Two in the Magic City, Paris, ca. 1931

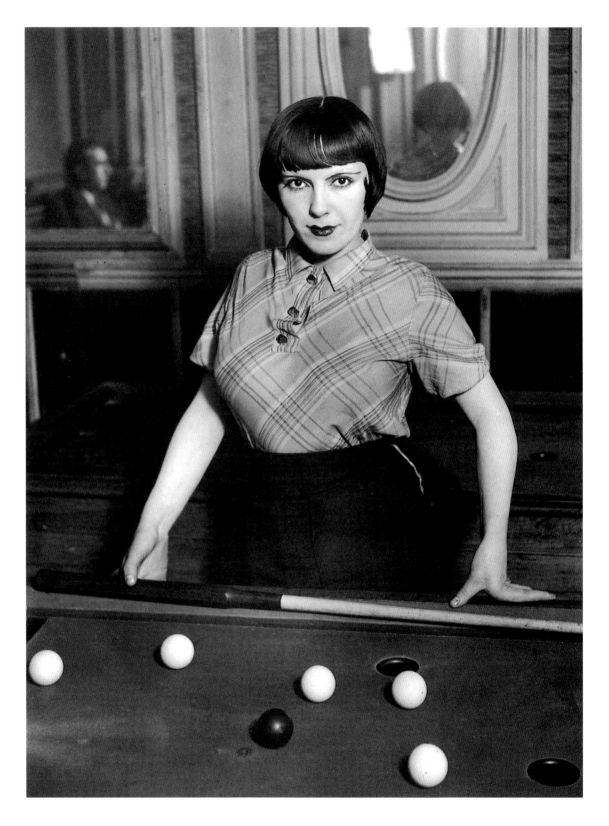

Billiards, Boulevard du Rochechouart, Montmartre, ca. 1932

22

WALKER EVANS

Walker Evans embodied the dispassionate, objective eye par excellence, soberly recording the architecture of New England, impoverished itinerant laborers in the Deep South, and passengers in the New York subway.

WALKER EVANS

1903   Born in St. Louis, Missouri

1922–1923   Studies at the Phillips Academy, Andover, Massachusetts

1926–1927   Visits Europe

1931   Photographs architecture in New England

1933   First solo show, at MoMA, New York

1935   Documents the exhibition *African Nego Art*, MoMA, New York

1935–1937   Commissioned by the Resettlement Administration (RA), in West Virginia and Pennsylvania, followed by the Deep South

1938   Begins his *Subway* series

1941   *Let Us Now Praise Famous Men*, with James Agee

1945–1955   Staff photographer, later editor, of *Fortune* magazine

1966   *Many Are Called*

1975   Dies in New Haven, Connecticut

The photographs collected in his most famous book, *Let Us Now Praise Famous Men* (1941), were taken on commission for the Farm Security Administration (FSA), a division of the US Department of Agriculture interested in obtaining an impression of the lives of the rural population, especially in the Deep South. Walker Evans focused on farmers and their families—especially children—the poor furnishings of their dwellings and their outward appearance, the fields and meager harvests. His lapidary stocktaking had nothing of the social reform agenda about it. Still lifes with family photographs and bric-a-brac on board walls, a white-sheeted bed, interiors with carefully arranged household goods, were masterpieces of the genre, taking the objective style of the 1920s and 1930s to a culmination. Not surprisingly, Evans's early pictures of show windows and interiors in New York and buildings in "old New England" occasionally recall the unpretentious realism of a Eugène Atget.

In 1938 Evans began photographing passengers in the New York subway with a concealed lens. The resulting portraits, of which the sitters were oblivious, were of a quite unprecedented kind: people lost in thought, unaware of being observed, their gazes empty, waiting without expectation. Out of discretion, Evans did not publish a selection of these images until 1966, under the title *Many Are Called*. The book represented street photography of a special kind, a panorama of anonymity and human alienation—an American counterpart to the "humanistic" photography of a Doisneau, Ronis, or Cartier-Bresson, whose insouciant charm glossed over the fact that we are all, ultimately, alone.

In his early forties, Evans made a name for himself at *Fortune* magazine, initially as a photographer, later with increasing editorial responsibility. During these 12 years emerged several series, including one of tools in sharp focus (*Auger Drill Bit with a Flared Screwdriver End*, 1955), and a color series on hydrants, street posts, and traffic and information signs entitled *Street Furniture*: expression of a prosaic realism far from all symbolic metaphor. Evans cautioned against the temptations of color photography, saying that "Many photographers are apt to confuse color with noise." Still, this did not prevent him from buying a Polaroid camera a year before his death ("nobody should touch a Polaroid until he's over sixty"), with which in one great splurge he shot over 2,650 more pictures of houses and sheds, interiors, people—and, of course, signs.

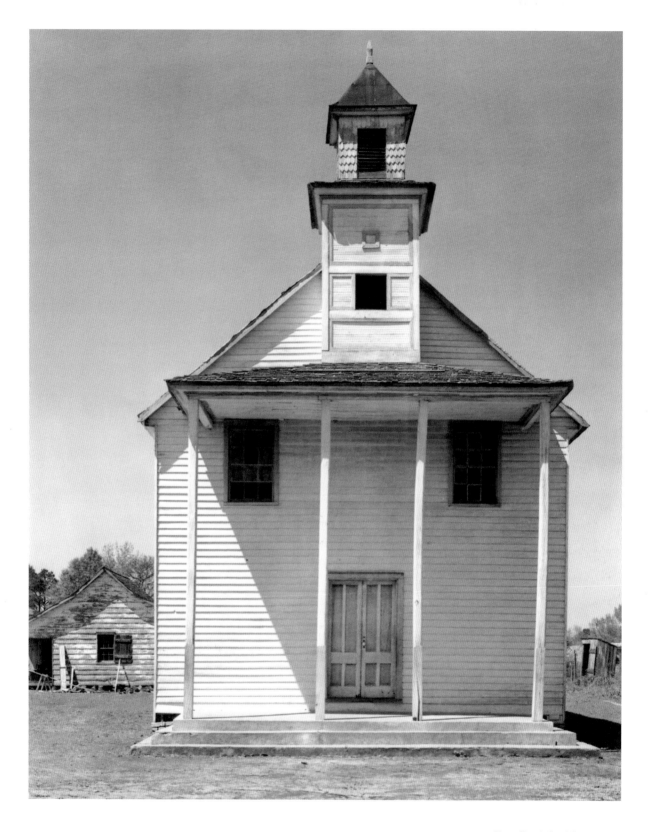

Negro Church, South Carolina, 1936

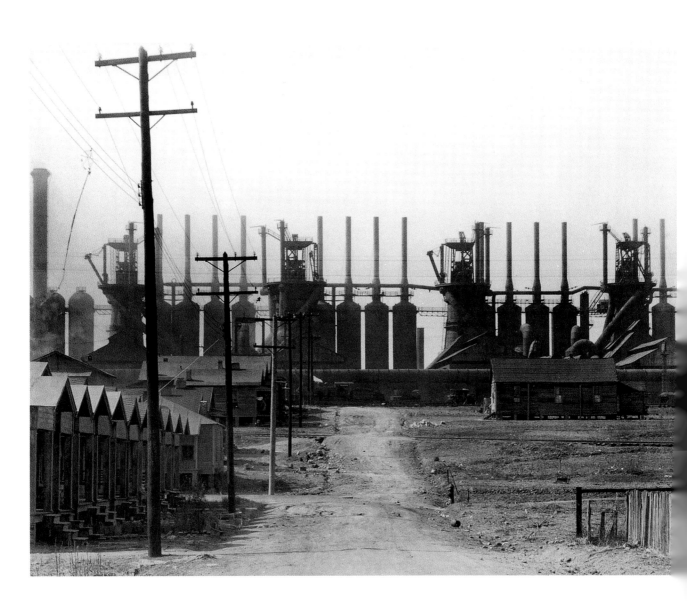

Birmingham Steel Mill and Workers' Houses, 1936

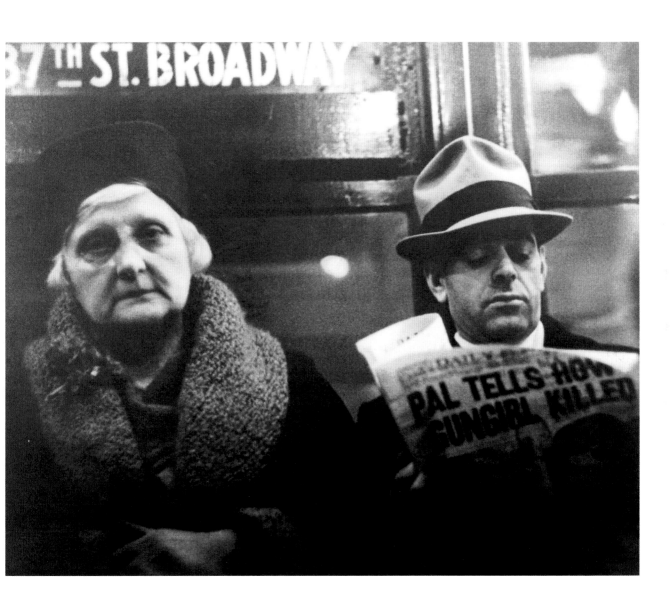

Subway Passengers, New York, 1938

23

ANDREAS FEININGER

Andreas Feininger was a tireless observer of New York: lunch-hour crowds milling along Fifth Avenue, the Empire State Building seen from across the Hudson River with the New Jersey meadows in the foreground, the cemeteries of Brooklyn …

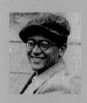

ANDREAS FEININGER

Unlike Weston and Evans, Andreas Feininger discovered the United States not as an American but as a newly arrived émigré. To his eye everything appeared gigantic, the country's wide-open spaces magnificent. His photographs of New York, Chicago, the East Coast, Florida and California were those of a perpetually astonished traveler. He recorded the harbors of New York, skyscrapers under construction, branching railroad tracks and elevated trains, the beaches at Coney Island and along the Atlantic coast. For Feininger, the enormous size and age of the redwood trees and bristlecone pines made them Californian monuments, and on the way there he captured the humble sights along Route 66, small towns with their filling stations, motels, and outgrowths of signs. Death Valley, Yellowstone, Pueblo Acoma, the great dams … avoiding postcard clichés, Feininger discovered a new world, of lakes freezing over, beaver dams, a cave entrance with hosts of bats flying out of it.

Having studied at the Bauhaus and worked in Le Corbusier's studio, Feininger tended to prefer architecture over people as a subject. It is noteworthy that as well as well-known buildings he photographed modern housing developments (*Van Nuys Gardens* and *Valejo*, both in California, 1947), the no-man's land of parking lots (*Houston, Texas*, 1947), and industrial plants (Standard Oil, Baton Rouge, Louisiana). The Signal Hill oilfields in California provided a contemporary counterpart to the redwoods.

In parallel, Feininger tirelessly investigated nature. Linking up with Man Ray, he experimented with solarization, the photogram, or a combination of these techniques, placing oak leaves, dragonfly wings, and other transparent objects in the enlarger or directly on photopaper. As early as 1939, a selection of these studies appeared under the title *New Paths in Photography*.

Close-ups of seashells were styled "goddesses of victory," or "ancient Roman architectures." Devilfish bones metamorphosed under the photolamps into monuments whose beauty, Feininger thought, surpassed that of many a modern abstract art work. He focused on beetle tunnels in tree bark, on grasses, on ice crystals on window panes, convinced that design was not only a human activity but occurred in nature as well. Feininger's aesthetic sensibility opened new fields for photography. Using apparatus he developed himself, he took macrophotography to a creative highpoint. He tempered the New Objectivity of the 1920s with imagination, built a bridge between nature and technology, and—very much the Bauhaus teacher—he passed his experiences along to the next generation in textbooks on the grammar and syntax of photography.

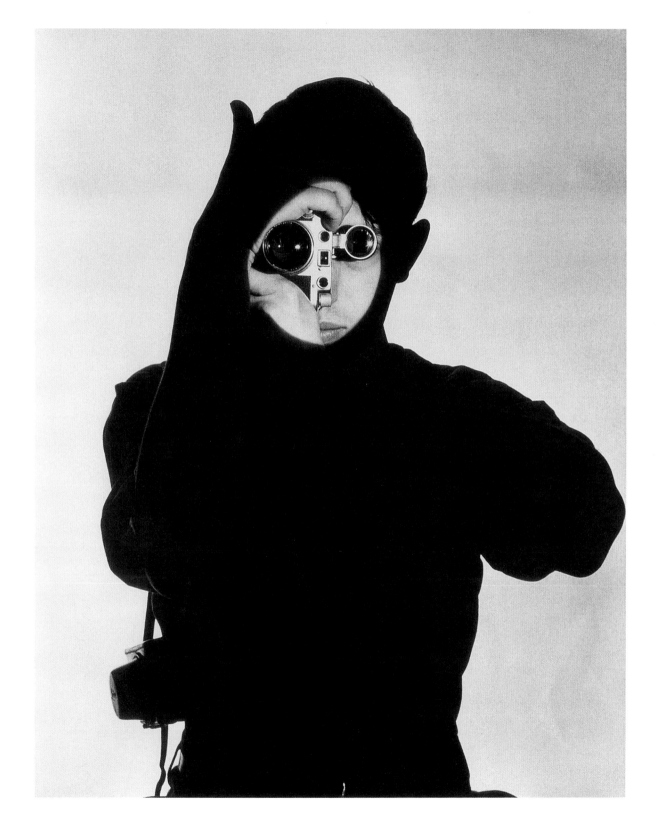

The Photojournalist Dennis Stock, 1951

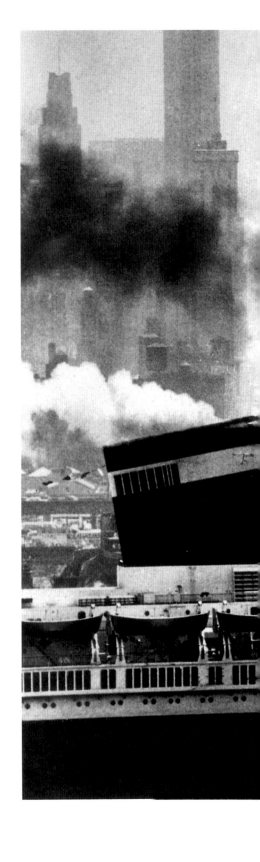

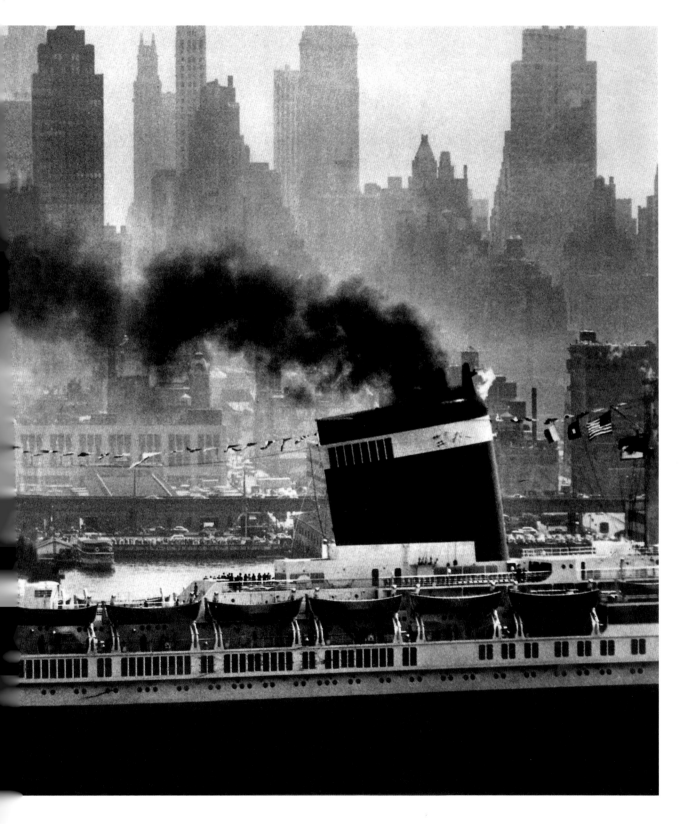

The *United States* Leaving New York Harbor for Europe, 1950

24

HENRI CARTIER-BRESSON

With apparent effortlessness, this "Raphael of photography" shot one masterpiece after another during the heyday of photojournalism.

HENRI CARTIER-BRESSON

Of the 96 years of his life, Cartier-Bresson devoted half a century to photography, and if he had not succumbed to the temptation of seeking recognition as a painter and draftsman in his old age, this period would have been even longer. "The eye of the century," as Pierre Assouline called him, was an incomparable eyewitness and observer: "It makes one shudder to imagine what all this eye has seen." Cartier-Bresson captured the world in a veritably encyclopedic way. With somnambulistic sureness he was often at places where history was in the making. He visited Mahatma Gandhi shortly before his assassination, and recorded an India in agony (1948). In China, he witnessed the last six months of the Kuomintang government and the victory of Mao Zedong (1949). In Indonesia, he was on the spot as the country was throwing off Dutch colonial rule (1950).

Active for two decades for the Magnum cooperative, which he co-founded in 1947, Cartier-Bresson was a photojournalist, but this apparently light-hearted world traveler and *flâneur* was more than a reporter. He was an adventurer of vision, who not only traveled through countless countries but lived in some of them for a time, in order to gain intimate knowledge of cultures and peoples. He turned his large, childlike eyes not only on historically significant events but also on the vicissitudes of daily life. A gentleman photographer, he detested making his own prints, and entrusted this darkroom work to others.

No other photographer left behind so many icons of the medium as Cartier-Bresson. Take the picture of those two gentleman of Brussels, covertly peeping through holes in a canvas fence (1932), the hatted fellow jumping over a huge puddle behind St. Lazare Station (1932), the ladies of pleasure in Alicante, or—icon of icons—the boy with the bottles on Rue Mouffetard in Paris (1952). Or one thinks of Matisse, photographed in Vence as he was drawing a dove, and the wonderful portraits of Alberto Giacometti. How many timeless portraits Cartier-Bresson produced, of artists, composers, and writers—sometimes in an unobserved moment, sometimes in a studio session that would have done justice to a psychoanalyst's couch.

He was a habitué of the group around André Breton, high priest of Surrealism, and on friendly terms with Max Ernst, Michel Leiris, and Jacques Prévert. This background explains the meaning of the "decisive moment" in his work, that celebrated fraction of a second or chance instant that became Cartier-Bresson's prime accomplice. It is thanks to the English translation—*The Decisive Moment*—of his book *Images à la sauvette* (*The Decisive Moment*), published in Paris in 1952, that he became almost too exclusively associated with the "serendipitous moment"—the photographer as hunter, prowling the streets with his Leica. With his demand that photography be unplanned, unexpected, that it simply *happens* by chance, Cartier-Bresson provided a counterpart to Surrealist "automatic writing." "If you try to force something, nothing will come of it."

Yet what really counted for him was geometry, infused with musicality and a sense of rhythm. His formula of his art: "Mind, eye and heart must be brought into line." With this classic combination of feeling, rationality, and a clear eye, Cartier-Bresson became the major representative of "humanistic photography" in the 20th century.

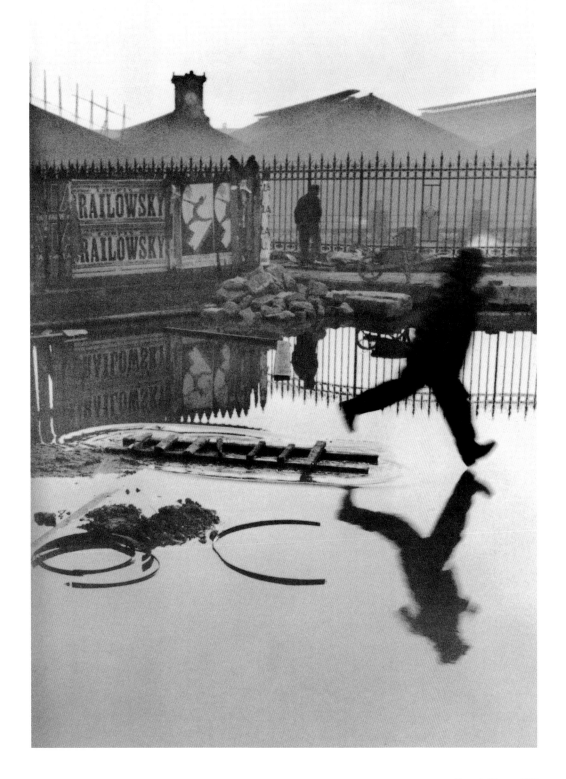

Place de l'Europe, 1932

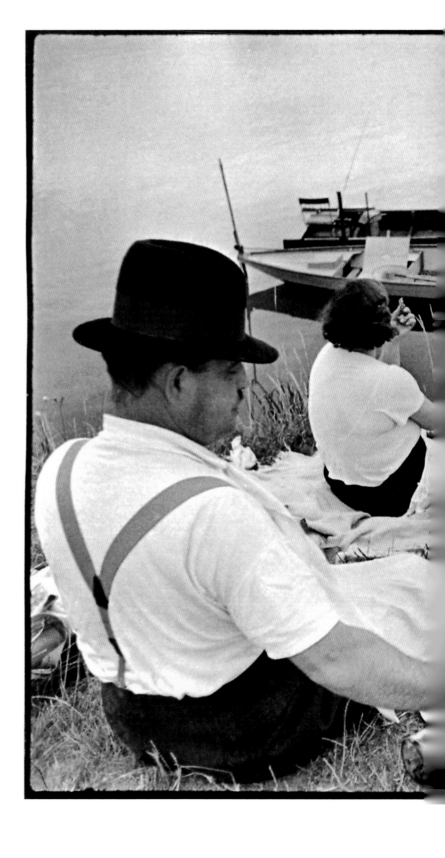

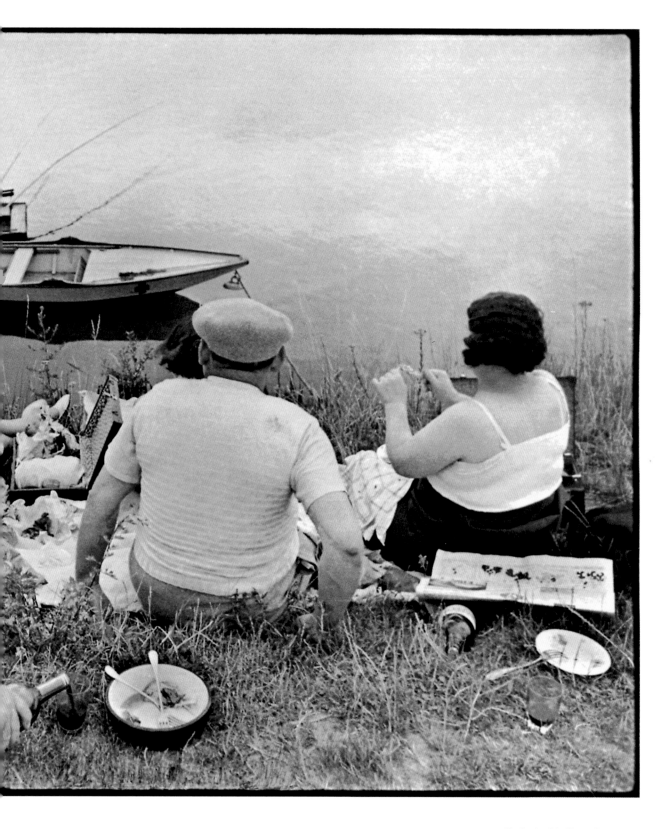

The Banks of the Marne, France, 1938

25 WILLY RONIS

Even at the age of almost one hundred, Willy Ronis remained a vital and humorous man. He always took the people in his pictures to heart, which explains the incomparable humanity that suffuses his work.

The photographs Willy Ronis took in Paris add up to a *voyage sentimental* through half a century, "a living memory," as Henri Raczymow put it, "our own, that of our parents, and that of our grandparents." Willy Ronis's special interest was in people he met in the streets: tradesmen, market vendors, children. The Paris of gala receptions tended to leave him cold. He preferred to roam the quais and markets, the railway stations and parks, the bistros and cafés. He captured the after-work and holiday diversions along the Canal Saint-Martin, the banks of the Marne, and other popular outing destinations. In 1947 he discovered the quarters of Belleville and Ménilmontant, whose unpretentious simplicity and poetry he memorialized in an eponymous book, perhaps Ronis's finest album.

Photography trips took him beyond the Paris city limits to the Vosges, the Alps (1937), to Limousin and Vivarais, to Greece, Yugoslavia, and Albania (1928–1939). After the war, Ronis traveled to Algiers, East Berlin, Prague, Moscow and Venice. "I don't arrange, I deal with chance," he once described his photographic recipe. While many of his colleagues were likewise in league with chance, Ronis never aimed at the humorous point—like Doisneau—or the classical composition—like Cartier-Bresson—but focused on the human aspects of unspectacular, everyday life.

Instructed in piano and violin as a boy and later animated by the desire to become a composer, musicality played a special role in Ronis's art throughout his career. In many of the compositions of this great admirer of Bach and Mozart, we come across structures reminiscent of polyphony. It is a combination of emotionality and rationality that makes Ronis' art special. As he himself once put it, "The beautiful image is geometry modulated by the heart."

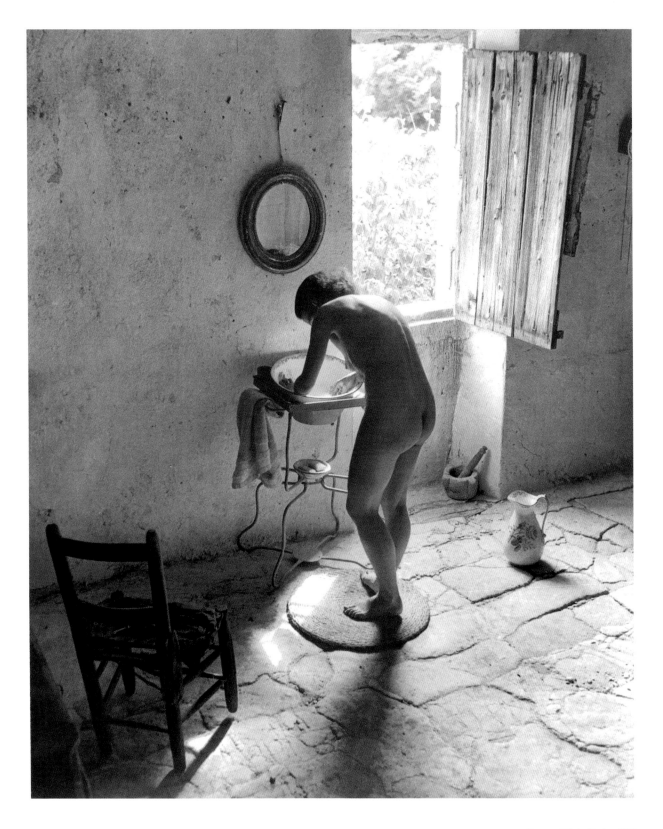

Provençal Nude, Gordes, 1949

26 ROBERT DOISNEAU

While other photographers were able to devote themselves to their original projects only in their spare time, Doisneau was fortunate enough to be able to use his many commissions for magazines and newspapers to pursue his favorite pastime: exploring Paris by day and night.

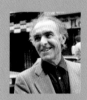

ROBERT DOISNEAU

1912   Born in Gentilly sur Seine, France

1926–1929   Trains as a lithographer in Paris, followed by work as an engraver and lithographer

1931–1933   Works as a photographic assistant to André Vigneau

1934–1939   Employed as a photographer for Renault

1939–1940   Serves in the army

1945   Becomes a member of the Alliance (Adep) photographic agency, Paris

1946   Works for the Rapho Agency

1948   *La Banlieue de Paris*

1949–1952   Regular contributor to *Vogue*

1965   *Epouvantables épouvantails*

1994   Dies in Paris

Like hardly another photographer, Robert Doisneau captured the *gaieté*, charm and nonchalance of the Parisians, even doing what he could to perpetuate this cliché. For his famous *Kiss in Front of Paris City Hall* (1950), done as part of a reportage on lovers in Paris for *Life*, he hired professional actors and posed them at various "typically Parisian" locations. Several attempts were needed before the scene looked "authentic." Although helping chance along on this occasion, he generally adhered to the following credo: "I always keep my foot a little in the door to let chance come in, pilfer something, or bring something I hadn't thought of."

Doisneau had begun his career with much less nonchalance, as a photographer for Renault, responsible for advertising, industrial, and product photography as well as graphic design, until the automaker fired him after five years for repeatedly manipulating his hated punchcard. Then, thanks to a continuous stream of jobs for French and American magazines, he became a chronicler of Parisian life. In parallel, he illustrated over 60 books with his photographs.

The beginning of Doisneau's career was overshadowed by the war. In 1940 he fled to Poitou, where he took refuge with a farmer's family. In several subsequent reportages he recorded life in Paris, which had come to a standstill under the German Occupation: empty shops, coal and food rationing, the severe winters. Then the city's liberation: the building of barricades, firefights, respites in the battle, and finally the entry of Charles de Gaulle. A year later, for the Communist magazine *Regards*, he recorded the plight of the *galibots*, child mineworkers—not with the social realism of a Lewis W. Hine in his famous series *Children at Work*, but an array of smiling kids, faces smudged with coal.

Soon the economic and cultural upswing brought a range of new subjects. In 1948—nearly 15 years before Ed van der Elsken's *Love in Saint-Germain-des-Près*—Doisneau made a reportage on the quarter that would lastingly shape the popular image of Existentialist bohemianism. A humorous culmination was a sequence on passersby transfixed by the oil painting of a female nude in the window of the antique shop owned by his friend, the part-time journalist Romi Giraud. Such reportages, or pictures like *The Last Waltz on July 14, 1949*, cemented the image of a perpetually and irrepressibly gay Paris in people's minds on both sides of the Atlantic. On commission from *Vogue* in 1948, a photo series on concierges emerged ("True concierges exist only in Paris..."). That same year, with Blaise Cendrars as author, Doisneau published *La Banlieue de Paris*. In both this series and his 1951 photographs of clochards (tramps), he struck a more thoughtful note, yet without transcending the boundaries of "humanistic photography." Among his most original creations was a series on scarecrows, published in 1965 under the title *Epouvantables épouvantails* (Scary Scarecrows).

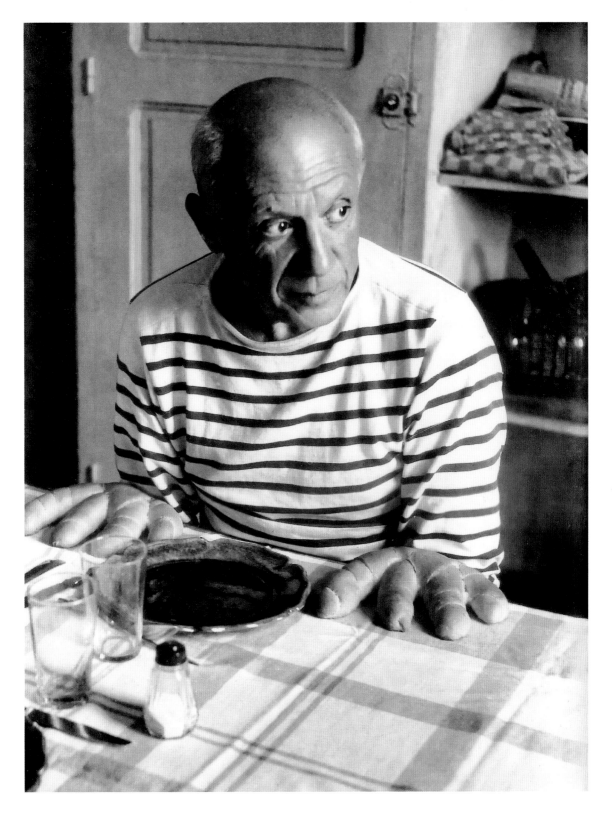

Picasso's Bread, Vallauris, 1952

ROBERT CAPA

Robert Capa recorded five wars, leaving him very little time for civilian subjects. He was the prime representative of a generation of photographers for whom political engagement, profession, and adventure were one.

As early as 1938, the English magazine *Picture Post* described Robert Capa as "the greatest war photographer in the world," before the Spanish Civil War—Capa's first campaign—had even come to an end. His reportages on the Japanese invasion of China (1938), on the Second World War (1941–1945), the first Arab-Israeli War (1948), and on Indochina (1954), were still to follow. And he was only 40 when he was killed by an anti-personnel mine in North Vietnam. Capa left behind over 70,000 photographs, made for *Life* and *Collier's*, the British *Weekly Illustrated* and *Holiday*, the Magnum Agency, and many more.

Many people thought he was a Spaniard, on account of his short stature and black hair. And his personality must have been charismatic, if even General Ridgway, Commander of the US 82nd Airborne Division, could write to the editors of *Life*: "Mr Capa, by reason of his professional competence, genial personality, and cheerful sharing of all dangers and hardships has come to be considered a member of the Division."

His images reveal not only Capa's mastery of the medium but his empathy and feeling of solidarity with the people he photographed: the Spanish Republican fighters and the victims of the civil war ruthlessly pursued by Franco and the Catholic Church; the Chinese child soldiers; Allied troops at the front in Africa, Sicily, Lower Italy, Normandy, the Rhineland. Asked how he managed to make the inhabitants of a Welsh mining region look so relaxed and natural in his pictures, Capa reportedly replied, "Like people and let them know it!"

Twice a refugee himself—from Hungary, then from Nazi Germany—Capa knew what it meant to be forced to leave a city or country. Wherever he went, he recorded the plight of displaced persons—fleeing from bombardments and advancing enemy troops, of the Japanese or Vietminh, or fleeing Israeli immigrants. He focused especially on the misery of children living in wartime.

Two of Capa's images have justifiably become especially famous. One is that of Federico Borrell Garcia, a member of the Republican Army, falling, rifle in hand, on September 5, 1936, near the village of Cerro Muriano, outside Córdoba. Known as *The Falling Soldier*, this image has become emblematic of the heroic courage of Free Spain. The second photograph shows a helmeted GI swimming ashore on D-Day, June 6, 1944, when the Allied invasion of Normandy began. This image embodies the bravery and sacrifices undergone by the Americans, the British and others as they set out to liberate Europe from Hitler's despotism. The two rolls of film Capa shot at the risk of his life on Omaha Beach were dried at too high a temperature by a laboratory technician at *Life* in London, causing the emulsion to melt. Although 61 of the 72 frames were ruined, the resulting blurred and grainy effect lent this one image its extraordinary effect.

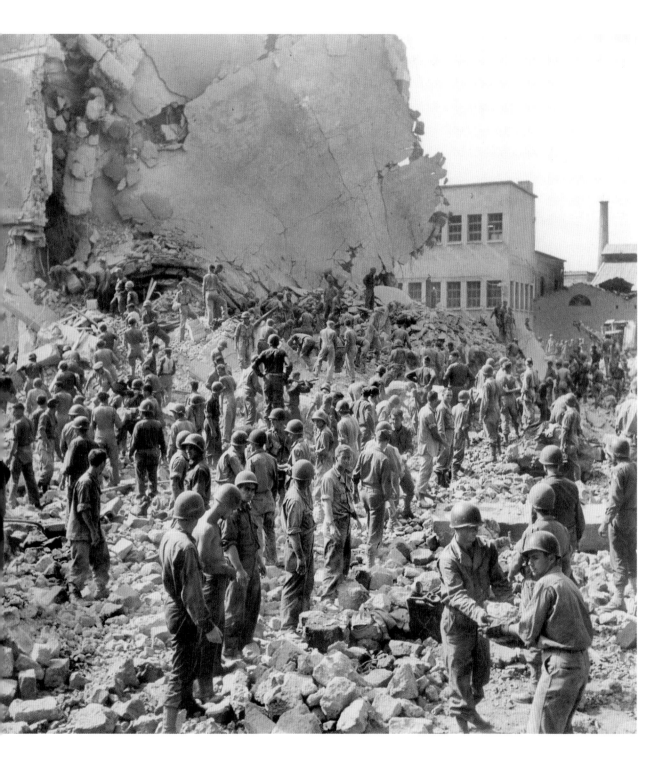

Naples, October 7, 1943

28

HELMUT NEWTON

The charm of Helmut Newton's photography lies in a sophisticated, exaggerated staging, suffused with irony. In some of his best shots, it seems he's making fun of the decadent world of illusion he himself helped to create.

HELMUT NEWTON

Considered the high-heel photographer par excellence, Newton worked with the highest-paid mannequins and extras, but not in the studio, because "A woman does not live in front of white paper. She lives in the street, in a motor car, in a hotel room." Miami, Paris and Beverly Hills were such locations, and Newton reputedly transformed his place of residence, Monte Carlo, into an open-air studio. Yet even more often than at exotic sites, he photographed in familiar surroundings or at places "no farther than three kilometers" from his hotel.

The effect of Newton's brazen nudes and semi-nudes derives from choice of setting, which frequently evokes a James Bond film, a road movie, thriller, or indeed a soft porno. There is doubtless a frisson in seeing females with cigars, handcuffs, and drawn guns, as if in some movie still, or in a leather corsage, in the role of *domina* or prostitute. Newton was also partial to the device of contrast, posing his beauties beside backhoes, tractors, or on a ledge above Hoover Dam—Amazons invading a man's world.

Renowned fashion houses commissioned Newton—a "gun for hire," as he jokingly styled himself—to photograph their new collections for the catalogues: Chanel, Yves Saint Laurent, Versace, Thierry Mugler, Blumarine. For other companies he did advertising, carefully respecting his clients' wishes and preferences. This commercial work gave him all the more freedom to do as he liked in his freelancing.

Newton also took outstanding portraits, of the Cardins, Ferrés and Versaces, but also of personalities such as Heinrich Harrer, Anthony Hopkins, Leni Riefenstahl.

Alice Springs once photographed her husband Helmut Newton clad only in a blouse, ladies' hat and pumps on the terrace in Monte Carlo, an image that perhaps more than any other attests to the humorously ironic relationship of the master of eroticism to such subjects, and to himself.

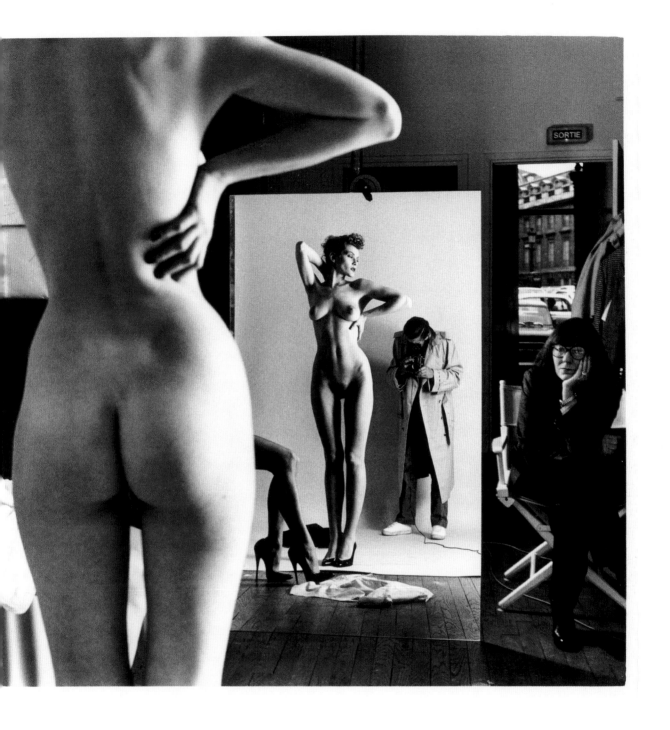

Self-portrait with wife and model, Paris, 1981

29

DIANE ARBUS

Initially a fashion photographer, Diane Arbus began freelance work at a relatively late date. Focusing on the human image, in the space of only 13 years she produced an oeuvre that is among the most penetrating and compelling of the 20th century.

DIANE ARBUS

1923 Born Diane Nemerov in New York City

1950s Works as a fashion photographer for *Vogue* and *Glamour*, with her husband, Allan Arbus

1958 Encouraged by her teacher, Lisette Model, she turns to freelance photography

1964 Receives a stipend from the John Simon Guggenheim Memorial Foundation for the project *American Rites, Manners and Customs*

1967 Exhibition *New Documents: Diane Arbus, Lee Friedlander, Garry Winogrand*, MoMA, New York

1971 Dies in Greenwich Village, New York, by her own hand

The career of Diane Arbus began with a sequence on an autopsied corpse with open ribcage, lying on a dissection table (1959). These images are emblematic of her merciless striving for truth in her approach to human reality. A familiarity with the photographer August Sander is reflected not only in her psychological portrayal of the people of her time, covering a great range of social groupings and individuals—the laconic objectivity of her portraits may also have been inspired by her great German predecessor. Yet Arbus left Sander's system of social classes and social etiquette behind to scrutinize the polarized America of the 1960s.

Again and again it is average people who seem to reveal most about the country: the boy in a straw hat, waiting to march in a pro-Vietnam War demonstration (1967); the kid with a toy hand grenade in Central Park (1962); or *Teenage Couple on Hudson Street, N.Y.C.* (1963). Normal families with children, elderly couples dancing or sitting on a park bench, a few celebrities, and a great many lonely outsiders were the people Arbus captured. And when the inhabitants of an apartment were unavailable, their living room furniture or a Christmas tree with presents in the corner told their story with equal eloquence.

"Everybody has that thing where they need to look one way but they come out looking another way," as Arbus once aptly described the fine fissure in our self-image, that "gap between intention and effect" on which her portraiture focused. "Scrutinizing reality"—she made no greater or lesser demand of her art.

Her images from the fringes of society perhaps did most to invalidate stereotypes. Arbus pictured transvestites applying make-up in their dressing rooms, celebrating a birthday, or with their hair in curlers; she photographed side-show performers, circus artists, and dwarfs; she attended dances for the handicapped. It was the rites of contemporary America she set out to record, the parties, contests, waiting rooms, theater rehearsals, initiations. The couple in *The Junior Interstate Ballroom Dance Champions, Yonkers, N.Y.* (1962), hardly more than children, reflect the potential of this superb project.

Paradoxically, yet quite logically, her images frequently include masked or costumed figures, her concern being to look behind the masks we all wear. A special twist on the unmasking theme was provided by the nudist camps Arbus visited several times—a world diametrically opposed to that seen in fashion photography.

Although she focused on individuals, her portraits convey general statements on the human condition. In view of the impossibility of taking pictures of everybody on the planet, she dared—by depicting individual idiosyncrasies—to convey the image of "a kind of generalized human being."

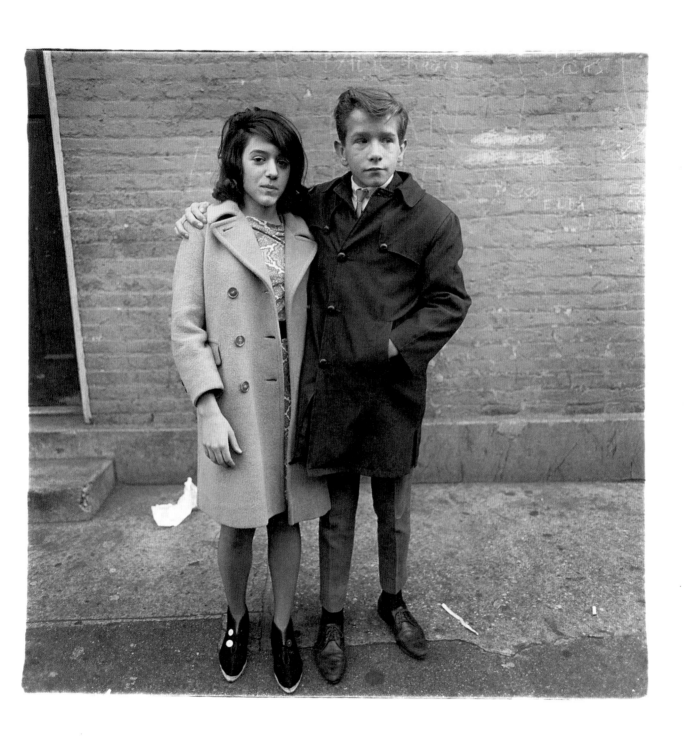

Teenage Couple on Hudson Street, NYC

30

RICHARD AVEDON

Already a celebrated photographer by the age of 22, Richard Avedon began taking photos for *Harper's Bazaar*, collecting awards and prizes galore. He was on the road again for *The New Yorker* when he died during a photo shoot. He was 81.

RICHARD AVEDON

1923 Born in New York City

1942–1944 Serves as a photographer in the US Merchant Marine

1944–1950 Studies under Alexey Brodovitch, at *Harper's Bazaar*

1945–1965 Works as the staff photographer at *Harper's Bazaar*

1947–1984 Photographs Paris fashion collections for *Harper's*

1962 Exhibits at the Smithsonian Institution, Washington, DC

1963 Photographs members of the Civil Rights movement

1964 *Nothing Personal*, with an essay by James Baldwin

1966–1990 Staff photographer at *Vogue*

1970 Travels to Hanoi, Vietnam

1976 Special issue of *Rolling Stone*: 73 portraits of the US political elite

1978 Retrospective at the Metropolitan Museum of Art, New York

1979–1985 *In the American West*

1992 Staff photographer, *The New Yorker*

2004 Dies in San Antonio, Texas

In his twenties, Richard Avedon had already achieved a success other photographers only dream of. Pictures of a street actress on Piazza Navona, taken in Rome in July 1946, of children in Trastevere and Palermo, marked his farewell to "everyday life" before his meteoric rise in the glamorous world of fashion tycoons and mannequins. For 45 years Avedon served as staff photographer, first with *Harper's Bazaar*, then with *Vogue*. For over 35 years he flew every summer to Paris to record for *Harper's Bazaar* the presentations of the great fashion houses.

Yet Avedon's true fame rests on his portraits. These unforgettable images include those of the contralto Marian Anderson (1955), the Danish author Isak Dinesen (1958), and the poet Ezra Pound, eyes tight shut (1958). His shot of Peter Orlowski and Allen Ginsberg embracing each other in the nude (1963) was just as scandalous as the group portraits of members of Andy Warhol's Factory undressing (1969). Then there was the shocking image of Warhol's stomach, scarred by a feminist's assassination attempt (1969).

Avedon's portrait style was inventive and monumental. He invariably attempted to show a personality from an unfamiliar angle. Without striving for effects, he often relied on compositional devices to look behind the cliché.

No one appeared more often in his viewfinder than his father, Jacob Israel Avedon. The resulting sequence is at once a unique document of the respect and admiration of a son after a period of estrangement, and a poignant record of ageing and physical decline. Avedon's exhibition of these portraits at the Museum of Modern Art in 1974 amounted to an homage both to his father and to the dignity of man.

Avedon's greatest portrait project occupied him for over six years. On the initiative of the Amon Carter Museum in Fort Worth, Texas, he took a portable white backdrop through 17 western states and photographed 752 people. As an exhibition and book entitled *In the American West*, the series caused a furor, showing average Americans from housewives, salesgirls and mine workers to butchers, and ranchers. Bill Curry, a drifter he met on Interstate 40 in Yuko, Oklahoma, appeared alongside the truck driver Billy Mudd, of Alto, Texas, and the beekeeper Ronald Fischer, his naked body covered with bees.

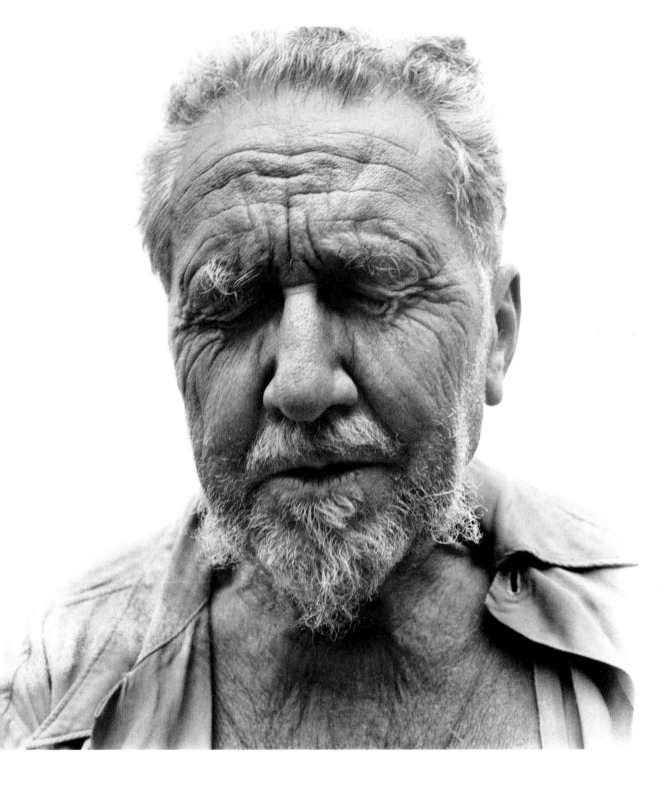

Ezra Pound, at the home of William Carlos Williams, Rutherford, New Jersey, June 30, 1958

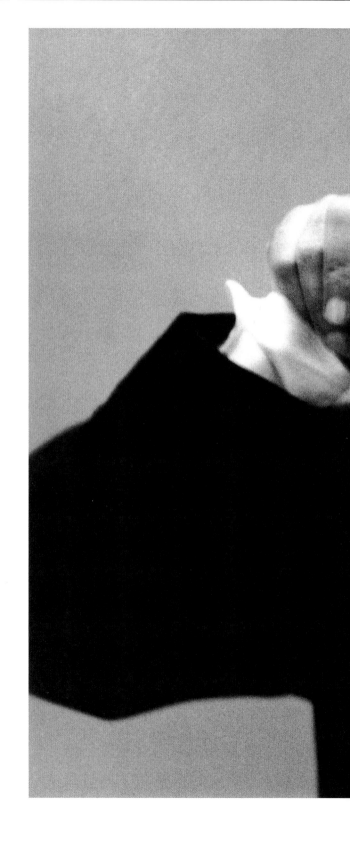

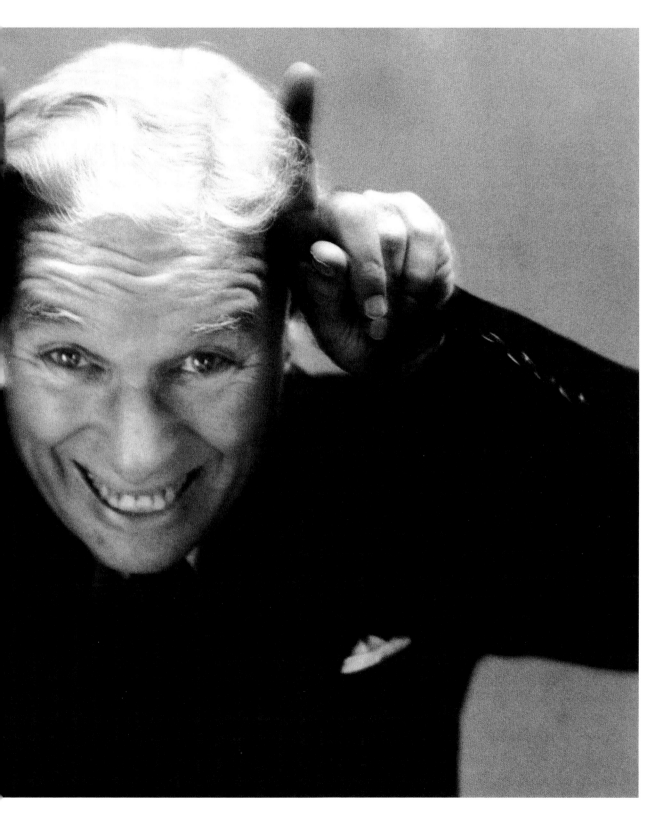

Charles Chaplin leaving America, New York, September 13, 1952

31

SEYDOU KEÏTA

"The August Sander of West African photography," Seydou Keïta, a key figure in the golden age of African portraiture, created a body of work which amounts to a single great portrait of society in French Sudan, which celebrated its independence in 1960 as the Republic of Mali.

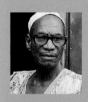

SEYDOU KEÏTA

1923 Born in Bamako, Mali

1948 Opens his own photographic studio on his father's premises

Early 1960s Works for the Sûreté Nationale (until 1977)

1993 Retrospective: Fondation Cartier pour l'art contemporain, Paris

1994 Participates in *1ères Rencontres de la Photographie Africaine*, Bamako

1996 Retrospective: National Museum of African Art, Smithsonian Institution, Washington, DC

1996 Represented in the exhibition *In/sight: African Photographers, 1940 to the Present*, Solomon R. Guggenheim Museum, New York, and numerous further exhibitions across Europe

2001 Dies in Bamako

During the final years of French colonial rule in West Africa, and thus of white-run portrait studios, local people began to take the place of their former mentors and provide photographs "by Africans for Africans." Seydou Keïta began with a simple box camera and basically taught himself the craft of photography. It was a Frenchman, Pierre Garnier, who encouraged him to develop his films and make his own prints. At 25 he opened a studio, complete with electric light, still a rarity at the time. Soon Keïta was in great demand as a portraitist of the bourgeoisie, and his reputation spread far beyond the region. The citizens of French Sudan—individuals, couples, families, groups of friends—posed for his camera in their Sunday best, complete with an array of status symbols.

Keïta's portraits are characterized by great care in the choice of accessories. With a fine sense of decorative effect, he posed his sitters in front of elaborately patterned fabrics that transform the portraits into luxurious interiors. These backgrounds combined with the vivid patterns of the sitters' attire to evoke dazzling "tapestries," an image of urban opulence and sophistication on the eve of independence. It was Keïta's aesthetic refinement that set his portraits off from those of his colleagues Abdourahmane Sakaly (Mali), Cornelius Y.A. Augustt (Ivory Coast), James K. Bruce-Vanderpuye (Ghana), and Narayandas V. Parekh (Kenya).

Keïta was the only one of these early African portraitists to use 13 x 18 cm flat negatives, from which he generally took contact prints and made enlargements when the client so desired.

Due to the high cost of equipment and materials, none of the representatives of the first generation of African portrait photographers were able to extend their activities beyond commissioned work. Keïta's oeuvre as we now know it originated in the late 1940s and the 1950s. In the early 1960s, he entered the employ of the Sûreté Nationale. His work for this institution remains publicly inaccessible. Keïta retired in 1977. It is thanks to the research of André Magnin that his work, after years of obscurity, was brought to light during Keïta's lifetime and earned him great international recognition.

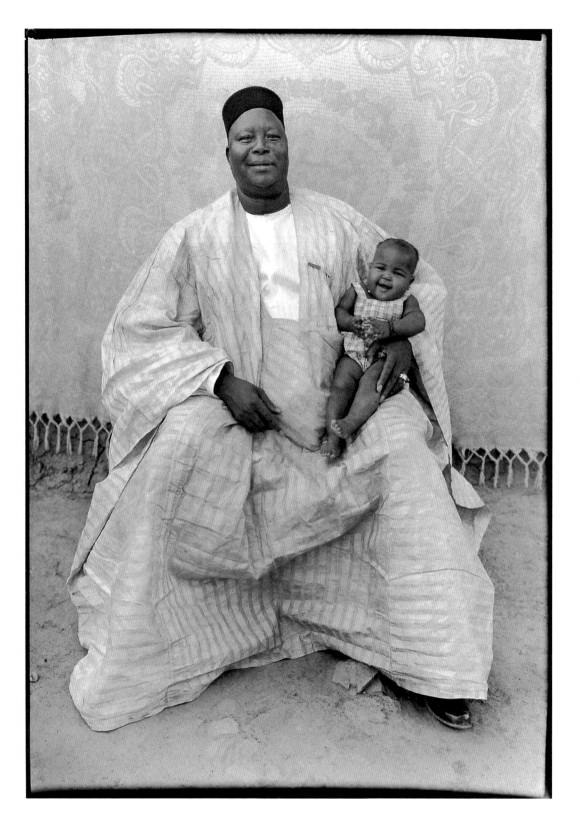

Man in Wide Boubou with Daughter, Bamako, 1950–1960

32

ROBERT HÄUSSER

At a time when few in Germany dared to give photography the status of an art, Robert Häusser made it absolutely clear that he considered himself an artist. He called his works "photographic images," precluding any association with random snapshots.

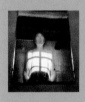

ROBERT HÄUSSER

1924 Born in Stuttgart, Germany

1940 Takes first photographs

1941–1942 Attends the College of Graphic Arts, Stuttgart; serves in the army and becomes a prisoner of war

1946 Settles at his parents' farm in Mark Brandenburg

1950–1951 Studies at the School of Applied Art, Weimar

1951 Sets up his own studio in Mannheim; jobs for industry and in advertising; numerous commissioned trips through Europe, to North and South America, and East Asia

1972 Begins concentrating solely on freelance work

2013 Dies in Mannheim, Germany

In retrospect, the abstract titles Robert Häusser gave his works were not necessary to underscore their artistic character: *Relative Orientations* (1972) for the picture of a street with white markings and reflecting posts; *Lost Place* (1982) for a brick façade with walled-up entrance. Works from his "Bright Period," which followed upon the dark pictures taken in a rural environment during the war and reconstruction years, drew their charm from many a fleeting moment and a fascination with serial structures typical of the period of "Subjective Photography."

Later, nothing lay further from Häusser's mind than momentary impressions. His images were built with a truly architectural solidity. A sonorous black is set against bright textures, and the range of halftones reduced. Häusser is a master of minimalism, focusing on only a few objects and lending them monumentality. He is intrigued most by massive, cubic forms. Yet he avoids a purely abstract play of forms by means of backgrounds reminiscent of Italian Metaphysical Painting or Surrealism. In his self-portrait (1981), he looks like an actor on stage.

Objects concealed under cloth, such as a concert piano or Jochen Rindt's race car after his fatal accident (1970), reflect Häusser's Magic Realism at its best. It was no coincidence that he always felt attracted to cemeteries, like Père Lachaise in Paris (1957), in San Miniato (1981) and Staglieno (1982), as they provided ideal sites for a combination of Cubism and symbolism. Animals appear in his work either dead and skeletized or as cadavers hung on hooks. With a hermetic approach not dissimilar to Josef Sudek's, Häusser attempted to set something timeless against the increasing secularization of society. Ordinary everyday life is almost completely excluded from this static world. People appear—as if in continuation of August Sander's approach—as representatives of occupations: *Musician* (1958), *Fishmonger* (1959), *Head Waiter* (1963), *Racing Driver* (1967). In addition, Häusser created a series of remarkable portraits of artists and art dealers.

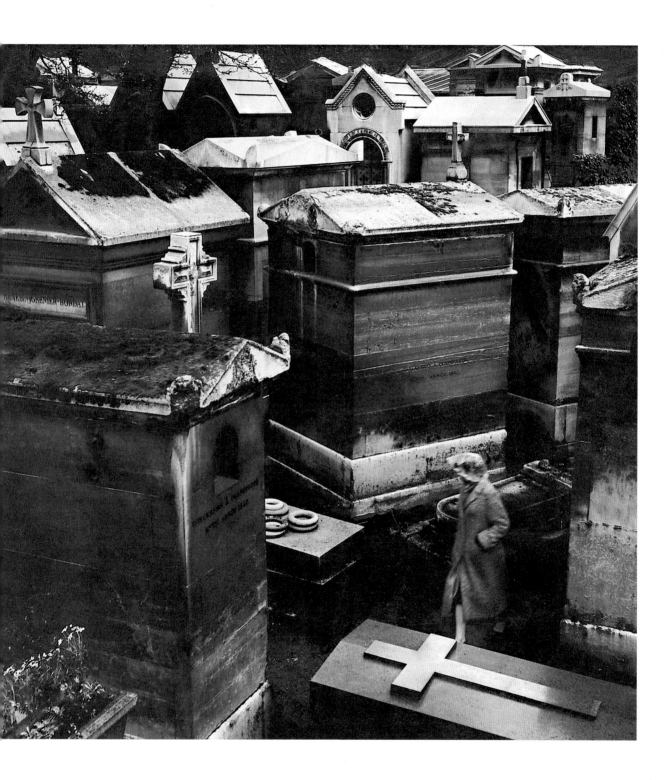

Cimetière I. Classe, 1957

33 ARA GÜLER

As a correspondent, Ara Güler traveled the world, portraying celebrities, the architecture of Sinan, the greatest of all Ottoman architects, and, his favorite motif—Istanbul—creating a unique homage to the city.

ARA GÜLER

1928 Born in Istanbul, Turkey, the son of an Armenian pharmacist

1950 Trains as an actor, then studies economics, and photographs for the newspaper *Yeni Istanbul*

Until 1961 Works as chief photographer for the magazine *Hayat*, then Near East correspondent for the new Turkey office of *Time-Life*, later for *Paris-Match* and *Der Stern*

1961 Becomes the only Turkish member of the American Society of Magazine Photographers; from 1951, works as a correspondent of Magnum, Paris

From 1975 Takes portraits of Bertrand Russell, Winston Churchill, Picasso, Dalí, and many others

1980 *Ara Güler–Photographs*

1989 *The Movie World of Ara Güler*

1992 *Sinan, Architect of Soliman the Magnificent*; photographs for the book *Living in Turkey*

1994 *A Photographical Sketch on Lost Istanbul*

Ara Güler lives in Istanbul

If New York is associated once and for all time with the photographs of William Klein, Paris with Atget, Kertész, Brassaï, Doisneau, and Ronis, no one will be able to think of Istanbul in future without recalling Ara Güler. He is known as the city's keenest eye, not as a chronicler or archivist but as a man who walked its streets and observed all its goings on. Güler's Istanbul is the city of dockworkers and porters, water and tea vendors, fishermen and artisans; his style a social realism that sees working people not as a class but as inhabitants of a city, and in consequence does without Marx and Engels.

One of his favorite haunts was Galata Bridge and the nearby neighborhoods, and he recorded life in Eminönö before it was razed in 1959. Just as Atget avoided the grand boulevards of Paris, Güler provided a picture of "old Istanbul"—its horse-drawn carts and slow barges, when hammer blows still echoed from the docks and the traffic-tailored, high-rise modern city and nationalism were still a thing of the future. His images spirit us nostalgically back to a time when you could walk past "garden gates covered with the purple flowers of the Judas tree." It is the Istanbul of fish restaurants, old Ottoman wooden houses, flaking façades—and poverty. Güler attempted to capture a "vanishing world," as he himself once admitted.

It may have been Brassaï's views of Paris by night that inspired Güler to wander the nocturnal city, collecting atmospherically charged images in the music bars and nightclubs of the popular Beyoğlu quarter. His pictures of ferries crossing the Bosphorus at daybreak, seeming to echo with the cries of seagulls, evoke the expanse of this metropolis spanning two continents. From 1950 to 1990—before the economic boom in Turkey set in—Güler followed the development of his home city in photographs, collecting the masterpieces from these four decades in the 1994 volume *A Photographical Sketch on Lost Istanbul*.

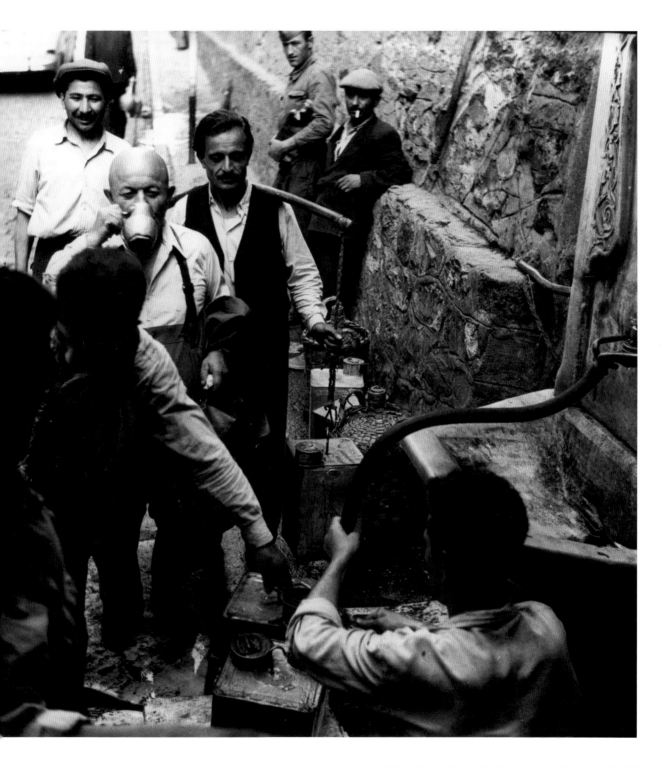

Water Sellers at the Hamidiye Fountain near the Galata Seraglio, 1952

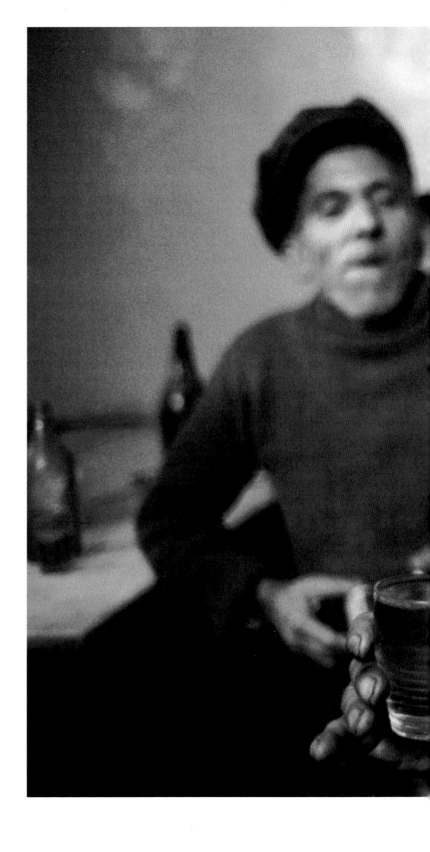

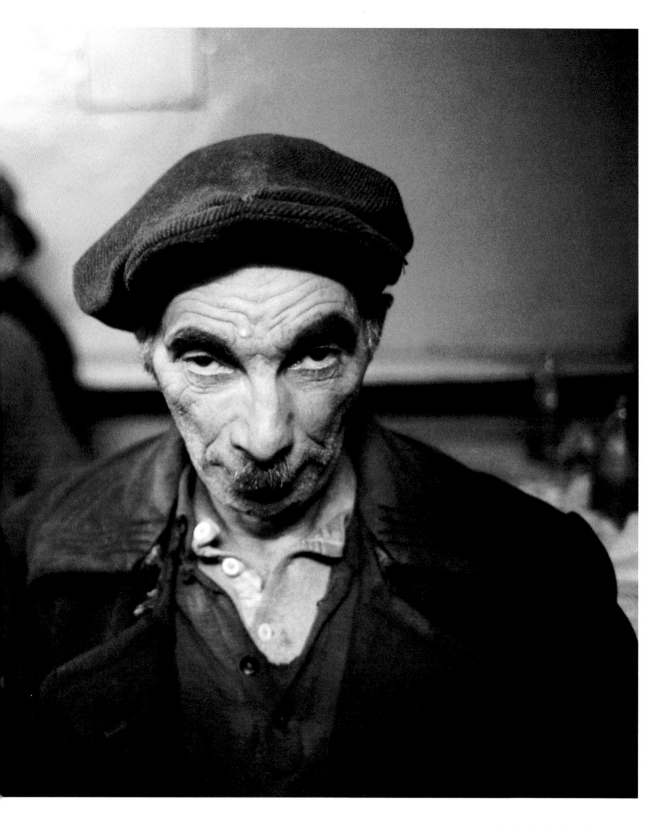

Drunken Man in a Bar in Tophane, 1959

34 GARRY WINOGRAND

The sites of Winogrand's compelling photographs range from the New York club El Morocco to the zoo, from the boxing world to the rodeo. He was the quintessential "street photographer."

GARRY WINOGRAND

When a city is still intact, its streets are not merely traffic arteries but places where people meet and greet each other, a theater where neighbors and passersby make their entrances and exits—the world stage begins right outside our front door. Garry Winogrand viewed this stage from ever-different angles, exchanging the psychologist's lens for that of the amused *flâneur* or the social commentator. He focused just as much on street artists and parades with acrobats performing on a trampoline as he did on random, anecdotal moments, looking passersby in the face or capturing their hurrying steps in experimentally daring excerpts. Yet unlike William Klein, he kept a respectful distance.

Equally diverse are the images Winogrand collected on the road during cross-country trips. He found motifs even in curves of the highway, house driveways, on sidewalks, or glimpses into an open convertible. Many of these pictures add up to an anatomy of American society. Those taken in the late 1960s in particular reflect a country divided against itself, when a state dinner for the Apollo 11 astronauts and upper-class balls and receptions are followed by Vietnam demonstrations and election candidates' public appearances.

Winogrand was also very influential as a teacher, holding countless workshops, teaching at over a dozen colleges and universities, and serving as instructor in Austin, Chicago, and several institutions in New York.

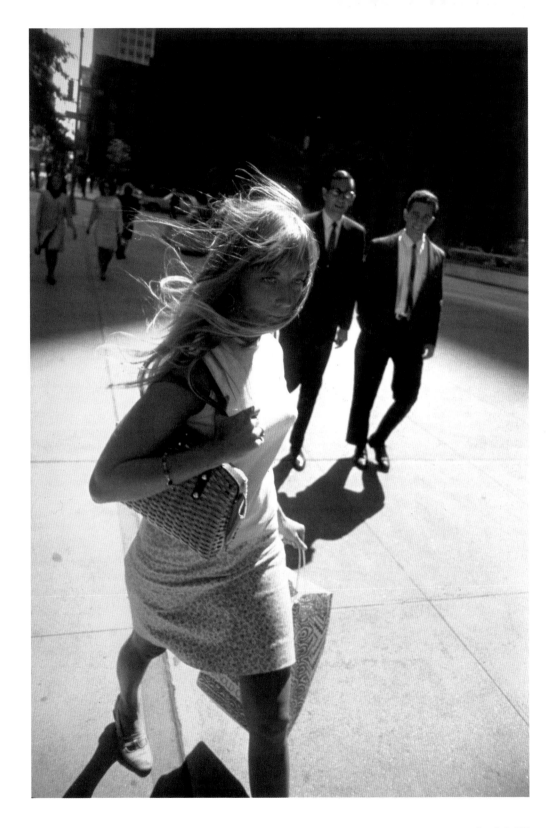

New York, 1965

35 WILLIAM KLEIN

People, people, and more people—for William Klein, the earth is a planet of human beings, who live packed together in New York, Rome, Tokyo, and Paris. He has devoted a book to each of these great cities, or rather to their inhabitants, and has missed hardly a public event in order to get as close to their stories as he can.

WILLIAM KLEIN

1928 Born in New York City

1947 Visits Paris for the first time as a GI; later, enters the studio of André Lhote and Fernand Léger

1954–1955 Takes photographs for the book *New York*

1955–1956 Takes fashion photographs for *Vogue*

1956 First winner of the Prix Nadar, for his photographic diary

1956–1957 Compiles images for *Rome*

1958 Begins series of over 20 documentary and feature films

1959–1961 Compiles images for *Moscow*

1961 Photographs for *Tokyo*

1962 Film *Les français et la politique*

1964–2002 Photos for the book *Paris*

1966 Makes the film *Who Are You, Polly Magoo?*

2012 Outstanding Contribution to Photography Award, Sony World Photography Awards.

William Klein lives in Paris

Compiled in 1954–1955, when Edward Steichen prepared and opened his exhibition *The Family of Man*, William Klein's book *New York* is a homage to the human turbulence of the metropolis. Klein combines extreme close-ups of faces with merciless excerpts, daring worm's-eye views with blurring. He brings us face to face with city dwellers who, young or old, are not put off by the camera lens and whose reactions to the photographer contribute much to the expressiveness of many scenes. It is thanks to Klein's communication skills that he was able to infuse "anonymous" groups of people with such life. Over the years he would make about 30 films (and over 250 ad spots), on Muhammad Ali, the Black Panthers, and many other subjects. The dynamism of his photographs already contained a seed of the cinematic. Klein denied both racial segregation and aesthetic categories. In his imagery high and low blend, signs, posters and billboards merge in the great visual melting pot of New York.

Over the following years he photographed in Rome, Moscow, and Tokyo. The city of Paris, on the other hand, though he knew it well and had an apartment there, he approached only with hesitation. Seen through the lens of hundreds and hundreds of earlier photo books, Paris initially seemed to him romantic, foggy, and above all monoethnic, a gray city inhabited by whites. When he finally began to focus on it, Klein discovered the city's modernity, its incredible futurism, by comparison to which New York suddenly looked old-fashioned. Using color film, Klein photographed crowds, demonstrations and riots, not to mention nightclubs, tournaments, and debutante balls. And then the funerals of Charles de Gaulle, Tino Rossi, Charles Trenet, and Yves Montand, with which, ironically, Klein opened his book. No other city, one gains the impression, could boast more civil courage and political consciousness than Paris. Interspersed images from commercial jobs for fashion houses add a note of profligate elegance.

This was Paris before the riots in the *banlieus* began, which made it clear that the inhabitants inside the periphery lived in a show window to the world and had almost forgotten the hordes of underprivileged immigrants around them.

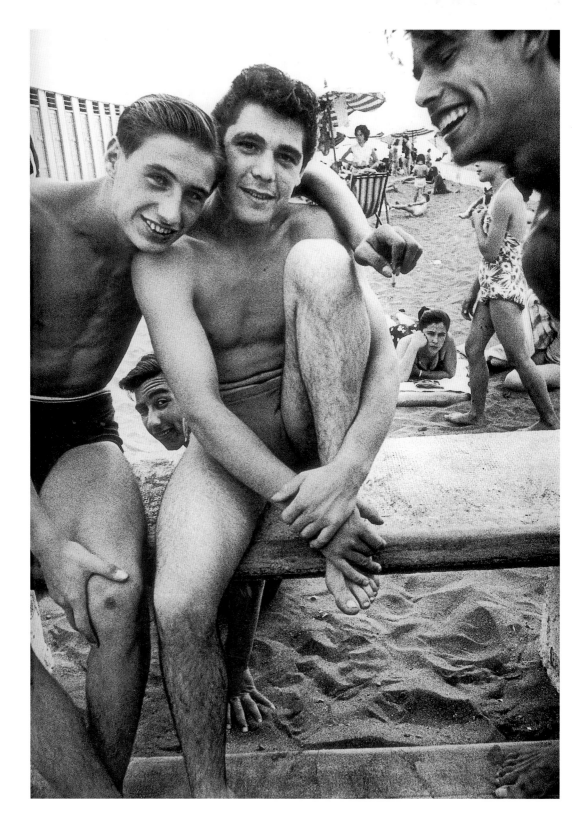

Plage D'Ostia, Rome, 1956–1957

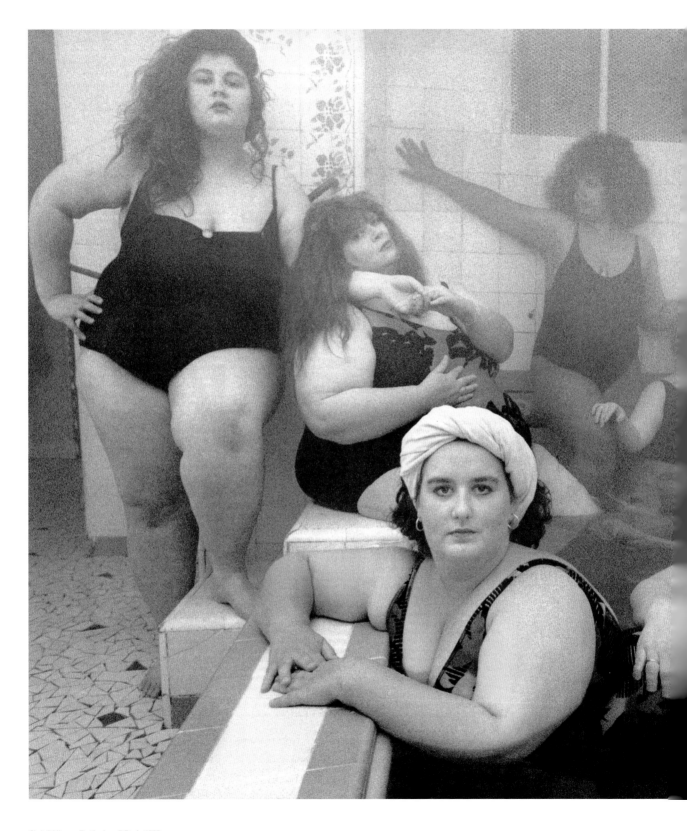

Club "Allegro Fortissimo," Paris 1990

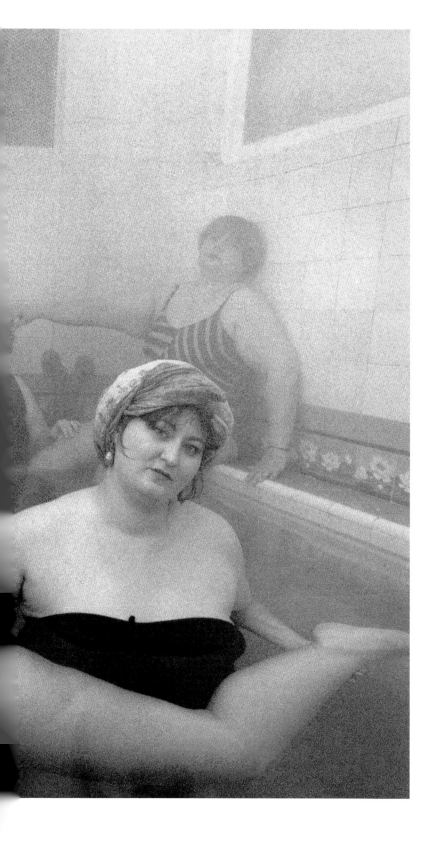

36

DAVID GOLDBLATT

No other photographer recorded South Africa under Apartheid with more psychological penetration. David Goldblatt crossed the borderline between the ethnic worlds to show how "South African structures are to be read the accretions of our history and the choices we have made."

DAVID GOLDBLATT

David Goldblatt was not a chronicler in the documentary sense. He photographed neither racial violence nor political events, but supplied—as a white South African—a social diagram of his country by focusing on its people, of whatever color. He attempted neither to confirm clichés nor to propagate social revolt, although he did greet the end of Apartheid with great relief. The quality of his images derives from the fact that, quite apart from their historical context, they represent magnificent studies of the human condition.

Goldblatt shows people at home or at work in a way that lends even the most ordinary of details eloquence. In his portrait of Miriam Diale in her bedroom in Soweto (1972), the elegantly dressed woman appears before an unpapered wall with a simple tulip-shaped lamp beside her. There could be no greater contrast than to the many living rooms of whites, which are veritably stuffed with mementos. Occupational portraits of blacks show domestic workers, cleaners, a broom saleswoman, a "boss boy"; those of whites a township superintendent, a chairman and business manager of a mining company. Although August Sander's occupational portraits reverberate here, an even closer parallel is seen with Diane Arbus's psychologically charged portraits from 1960s New York.

Goldblatt's masterworks include a series of photo reportages, especially the one on "shaft sinking" at the President Steyn No. 4 Shaft at Welkom (Orange Free State), images of great atmospheric density that reflect men's stamina under adverse conditions. This series is the South African counterpart to Salgado's much later photographs of a gold mine in Serra Pelada, Brazil (1986).

Even more unsettling are Goldblatt's 1983–1984 pictures of commuters from the homeland of KwaNdebele, who every morning at 3 a.m. boarded a bus for a several hours' ride to their workplaces in Pretoria and returned by the same route every night—permanent residence in white neighborhoods being prohibited by the Group Areas Act. Anyone who infringed this ruling risked a considerable fine or even prison, as reflected in Goldblatt's portrait series on punished individuals and families (1981). Entire housing developments, city districts and buildings were demolished when they were declared "black spots," and reopened for white settlement. In 1977 Goldblatt created a memorial for one of these areas, Fietas, before the razing of its private residences and commercial buildings began. Another series documented Protestant churches in South Africa, proving that towards the end of apartheid, the churches grew increasingly windowless and fortress-like.

The new South Africa also gave Goldblatt an opportunity to explore the "social landscape" and its faultlines. In large-format images he recorded historical places and landscapes redolent with the absurdity of white urban planning. A further series was devoted to views of streets "in the time of AIDS."

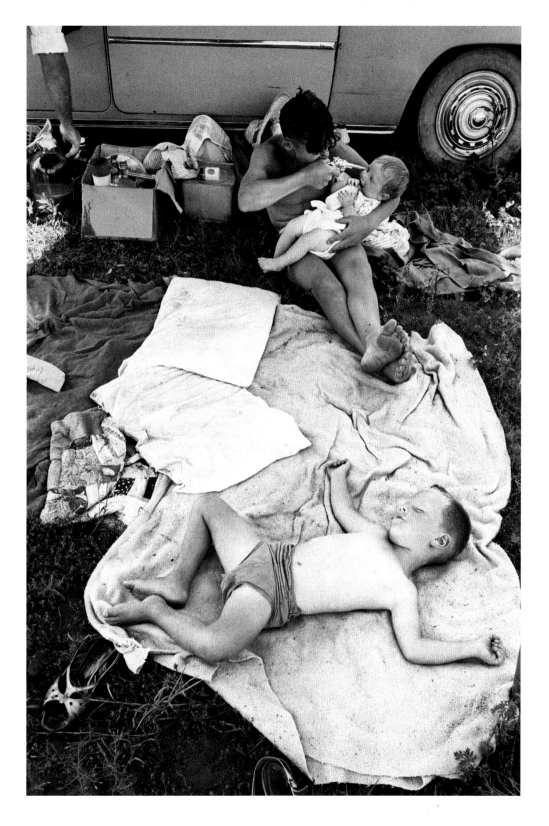

Picnic on New Year's Day, Hartebeespoort, Transvaal, 1965

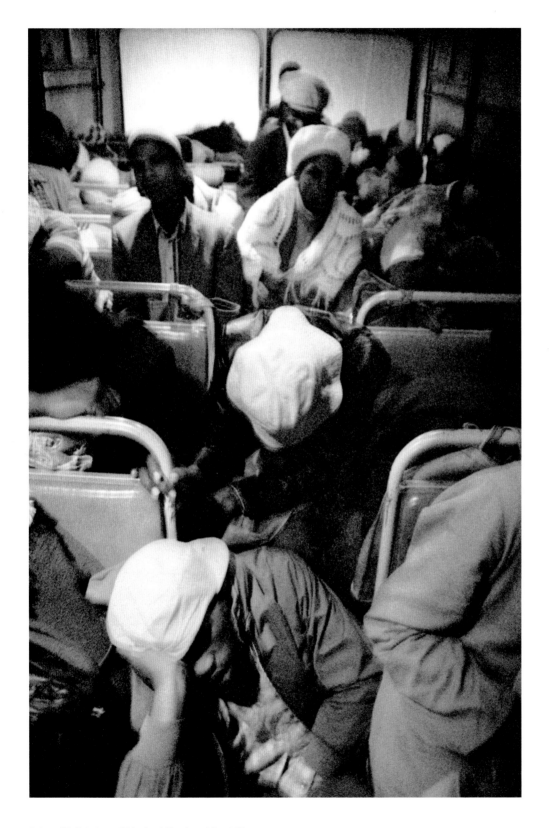

Going to Work: 3:30 a.m., Wolwekraal-Marabastad Bus, 1983

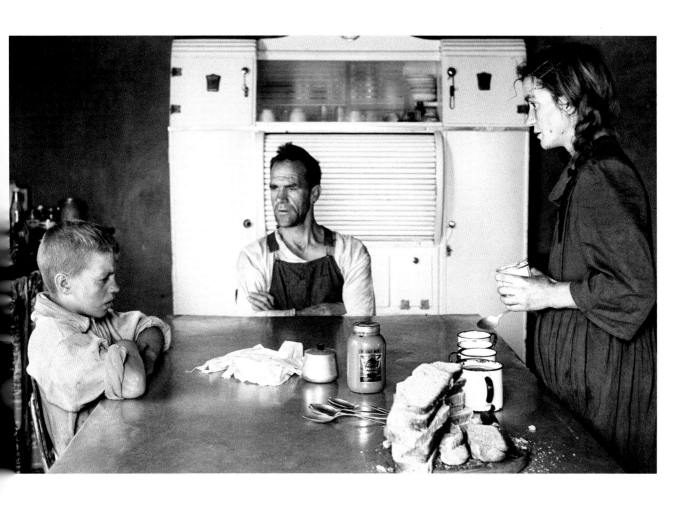

A Plot Holder, His Wife and Their Eldest Son at Lunch, Wheatlands, Randfontein, Transvaal, September 1962

37

BERND AND HILLA BECHER

The Bechers' encyclopedic oeuvre attests to an obstinate resistance to the ravages of time, to the imminent demolition and decay of abandoned industrial buildings.

BERND BECHER

1931 Born in Siegen, Germany

1947–1950 Serves an apprenticeship in decorative painting

1953–1956 Attends Stuttgart Art Academy

1957–1961 Studies typography at Düsseldorf Art Academy

1959 Starts collaboration with Hilla

1961 He and Hilla marry

2007 Dies in Rostock

HILLA BECHER

1934 Born Hilla Wobeser in Potsdam, Germany

1951–1954 Serves an apprenticeship in photography, then works freelance

1958–1961 Helps to establish a photography department at the Düsseldorf Art Academy

2015 Dies in Rostock

Pittsburgh, the Ruhrgebiet, Liverpool, Lorraine—world-famous manufacturing cities and regions that simultaneously call the great economic crises to mind. The decades-long decline of the German coal mining and steel industry not only put hundreds of thousands out of work but delivered up the concrete vestiges of a bygone era to the demolition ball. The architectural record of heavy industry on the Rhine and the Ruhr—former pride of the early industrial period—will remain part of the general visual memory thanks to the Bechers' painstaking collecting and recording activity.

For 40 years they roamed the region around Dortmund, Essen, and Siegen, photographing mines, pitheads, water towers, Bessemer converters, gasometers, ventilators and factories. They recorded grain silos and houses, especially the half-timber houses in the Siegen manufacturing area. Pilgrimages with the camera took them to abandoned manufacturing plants in Liège, Pas-de-Calais, Ohio, South Wales, and Pennsylvania. It was a systematic survey of a kind not seen since the days of Eugène Atget. Albert Renger-Patzsch, too, was a predecessor of this type of industrial reportage.

The Bechers' archival activity was sparked by a fascination with the commanding presence of these industrial monuments, their look of "anonymous sculptures," despite the fact that, being engineering structures, they were seldom designed with an eye to aesthetic effect. Their aim was "to prove that the forms of our times are the technical forms," as they announced as early as 1971. This was the period of Pop Art, when many artists, tired of subjective abstraction, turned to the cool gloss of the readymade and sometimes rejected painting entirely.

To achieve maximum precision, the Bechers used large-format cameras whose long exposure times caused passersby to vanish from the picture. Only diffuse, cloudy light supplied the homogeneous illumination they desired. Photographing in spring or fall had the advantage that shrubs and trees were bare and did not obscure the structures. The Bechers climbed ladders and scaffolds, perched on roofs, or photographed from the windows of neighboring houses to find the ideal, half-high vantage point from which images undistorted by perspective could be taken. This unchanging viewpoint from image to image engenders a regular rhythm that lends a compelling aesthetic effect to their photographs when combined into multipartite tableaux.

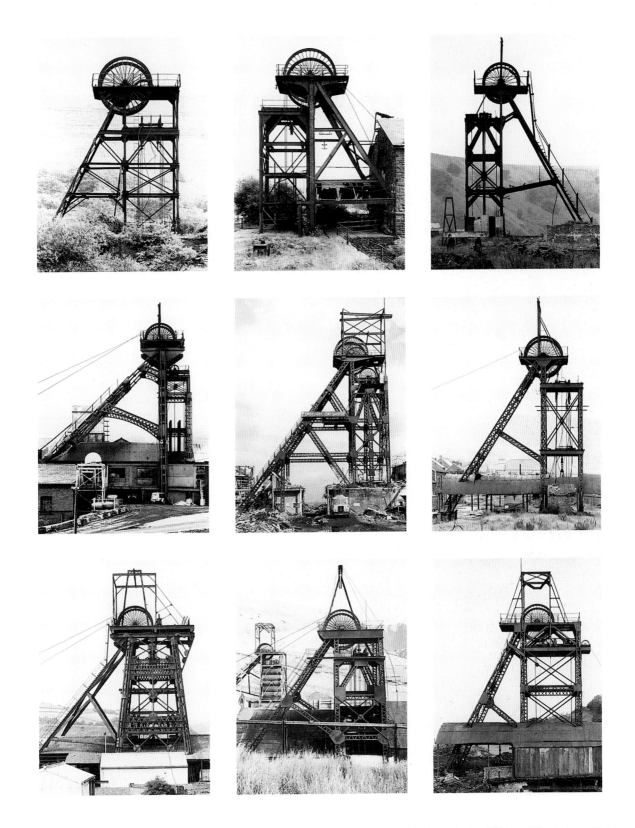

Shaft Towers in South Wales and Manchester, undated

121

38 BRUCE DAVIDSON

Bruce Davidson is best known as a photographer of the Civil Rights Movement in America. His sympathy for this cause was highly appreciated by black Americans from New York to the Deep South, and opened doors for him to their private lives.

BRUCE DAVIDSON

1933 Born in Oak Park, Illinois

1949 Wins the Kodak National High School Contest

1950 Attends Rochester Institute of Technology, then Josef Albers' class at Yale University

1955–1957 During military service, meets Cartier-Bresson in Paris; his first photos published in *Life*

1958 Becomes an associate member of Magnum

1959 Photoessay *Brooklyn Gang* published in *Esquire*

1961–1964 Takes fashion photographs for *Vogue*; accompanies Freedom Riders on an illegal bus trip from Montgomery, Alabama (1961)

1962 Guggenheim Fellowship for his work on the Civil Rights Movement

1963 Exhibits at MoMA, New York; photographs the construction of the Verrazano Narrows Bridge

1965 Photoessay *Welsh Miners*

1986 First color photo series, *Subway*

1999 *Portraits*

Bruce Davidson lives in New York

Bruce Davidson's early essay, *Brooklyn Gang* (1959), records the activities of the Jokers, one of the many New York street gangs notorious for their skirmishes. He went to Coney Island with these youngsters, where they spent the night under the Boardwalk. (His picture of a blonde girl combing her hair in the mirror of a cigarette machine would become famous.) Then they all took the bus back to Manhattan. Davidson was 24 at the time, the gang members 17. Though his photographs were rejected by *Life*, a year later they were published in *Esquire*. In 1962 they promptly earned Davidson a Guggenheim Grant, which enabled him to devote two years to the subject of "Youth in America." "I now had the youth from the Freedom Rides and the South on my mind," Davidson recalled, and he allied himself with those who openly opposed "the status quo of segregation, bigotry and intolerance."

Without adopting an accusatory tone, Davidson depicted the life of New York blacks on the lower rungs of the social ladder, demonstrations, the arrest of activists by the police, but also moments of joy in the black community. Characteristic of his style was a poetic suspension of moments in the flux of time. At public appearances of political leaders, such as Malcolm X in New York, he focused largely on the spectators. Pictures taken in Chicago in 1962 provided insights into the life of the black upper class. In harsh contrast were his photographs of the Georgia cotton fields, and of shacks in an itinerant laborers' camp in South Carolina with a school barracks for black children. A Ku Klux Klan nocturnal ritual made it graphically clear that the social air in America was ablaze.

In Davidson's photographs of protest marches in Mississippi and Birmingham, it was the scenes taking place on the margins that were especially eloquent. We should remember that these were the years when black activists boarded "white" buses despite segregation and severe risked a beating for it. On August 28, 1963, Martin Luther King delivered his "I have a dream" speech, and Davidson photographed the hope-filled masses gathered in front of the Washington Monument. Recalling the 54-mile (87-kilometer) protest march from Selma to Montgomery on March 21, 1965, the photographer said, "I walked with the marchers over the entire route, photographing many of them face-to-face. I wanted to see them as individuals, not just as symbolic silhouettes in a faceless crowd."

For his two-year project *New York: East 100th Street*, Davidson chose a block in Spanish Harlem which, neighbors said, was the worst in one of the city's most notorious slums. He worked with a plate camera and tripod, "to see with greater depth and sharper detail in to the rooms, buildings, vacant lots, streets and rooftops that define the space they called their home." Though these people trusted Davidson and gave him access to their private sphere, he was "afraid to break the painful barrier of their poverty." This project stands in the great social documentary tradition of a Dorothea Lange and Walker Evans, though with the focus shifted from fieldworkers' shacks in the Deep South to the tenements of New York.

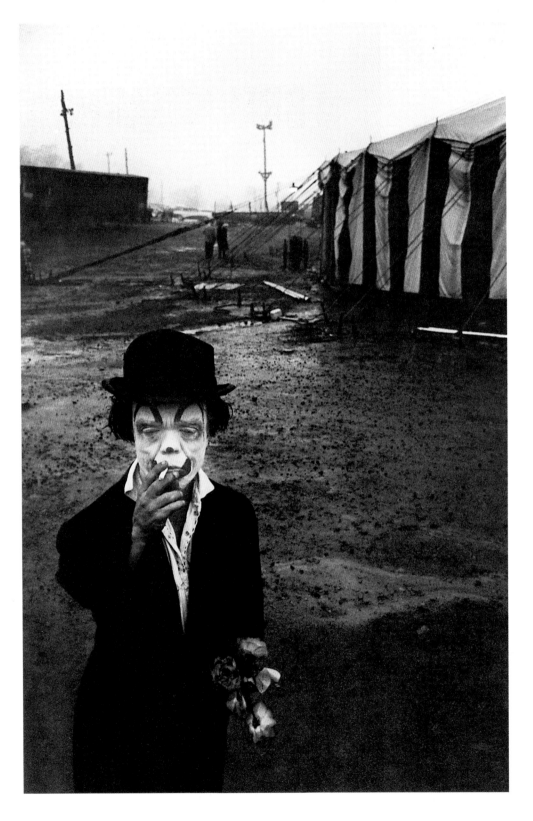

The Dwarf, Jimmy Armstrong, Palisades, New Jersey, 1958

39

RENÉ BURRI

> "What counts is putting the intensity that you yourself have experienced into the picture. Otherwise it's just a document."
> René Burri

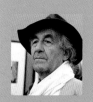

RENÉ BURRI

Like Cartier-Bresson, for over 40 years René Burri sought out the hot spots of world politics. Airplanes were his living room. He shot wars without becoming a war photographer, and he captured countless street scenes without becoming a representative of "street photography." He took photographs of Picasso and Le Corbusier, Giacometti and Tinguely, without ever viewing himself as a portraitist. In addition, for many years he focused on major modern buildings, yet in his freelance work architecture always took second place to people. Burri's work is most outstanding for a kaleidoscopic variety in which the transitions between the genres are well-nigh indistinguishable.

Averse to official posturing, he preferred the margins of big events or waited patiently for some unexpected private gesture that showcased the incidental—especially at state occasions, for which he had a season ticket. Burri was gifted at making subtle, humorous points that never descended to the level of gags. His masterwork is the collection *The Germans*, a grand tour through a divided and later reunited country, the diagram of a society composed of highly diverse impressions gained in East and West from 1957 to 1997.

It is tempting to associate Burri's aesthetic rigor with his Protestant Swiss background, and with the expectations of the Swiss journal *DU*, to which he often contributed. Extreme close-ups of faces and other such formal experiments were not his thing. Instead, he infused complex scenes teeming with figures with an intriguing ambiguity. This holds for *John F. Kennedy's Funeral* (1963) as much as for *Café, Tu-do Avenue, Saigon* (1973). Burri's finest shots show situations that are seemingly drifting apart or charged with tension, rapidly clamped into a unity as if by collage.

His most important portrait shows a cigar-smoking Che Guevara in an expansive mood, very relaxed by comparison to Alberto Korda's Christ-like icon. Burri's masterful photograph *São Paulo, Argentina* (1960) is a record of a torn society, taken from a bird's-eye view, overlooking the roofs and cavernous streets of the metropolis. Much as for his exact contemporary Lee Friedlander, for Burri the world could hardly be grasped through the truth of *a single* viewpoint.

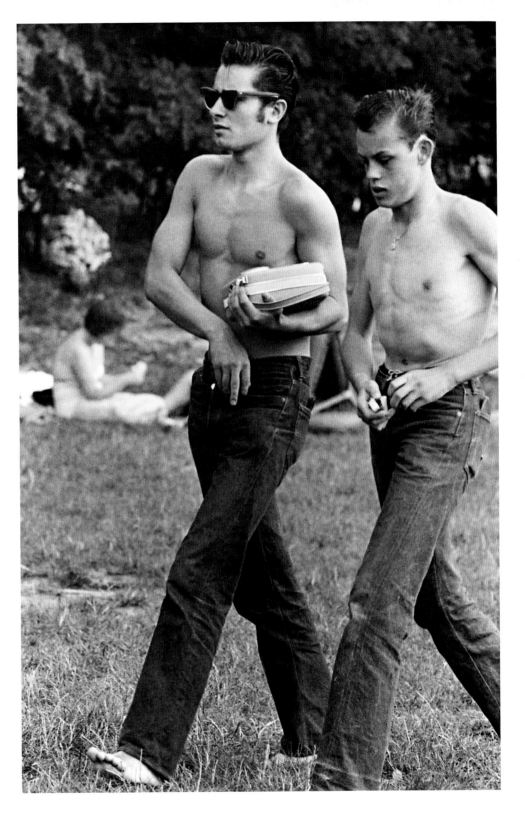

Wannsee Park, 1961

40

LEE FRIEDLANDER

Lee Friedlander is the master of urban collage, creating a provocative kaleidoscope of glimpses of the everyday aspects of the city. Yet as soon as we've become accustomed to the smell of asphalt he takes us into the great outdoors with its plants, trees, and landscapes. Never in deadly earnest, he enjoys playing jokes on his viewers.

LEE FRIEDLANDER

While other photographers avoided posts, streetlamps and traffic signs to gain an unhindered view of buildings, streets and passersby, Friedlander purposely let "street furniture" intervene. For him, advertising, billboards and signs were an integral part of the urban texture that made all modern cities look the same. People hurrying by—no longer the idle strollers of a bygone era—appear fragmented, part of the jumble of urban symbols. Mirrors and mirroring, reflections in display windows, maximize the visual complexity, and when a poster appears, our gaze seems to bounce back from it.

Friedlander photographed images of images, making obsolete the question of where reality stops and media reproduction begins. He fed his impressions of big cities into revolving glass doors, creating an equivalent to Robert Rauschenberg's "combine paintings." A chapter in his series *Architectural America* reduces Los Angeles, Phoenix, and New York to obscuring fences, and in another place most of what we see of "Nebraska," "Portland" and "Las Vegas" are the door handles and upholstery of his sedan. Friedlander's 1993 book *Letters from the People* is an updating of the random urban visual texts of the kind seen in Brassaï's 1930s graffiti.

His early portraits, no longer serving the illusion of great individuality, show people in their personal ambience or outdoors, often evidently tired and sometimes purposely unphotogenic. Usually in the worst mood of all is Friedlander himself—in unassuming, private self-portraits he grimaces because the camera is too close, or because taking his own picture perhaps wasn't such a good idea after all.

A tendency to sabotage pathos was already evident in Friedlander's 1970s series *The American Monument*. It showed American heroes in self-aggrandizing poses, mounted, imperially enthroned, fulfilling the country's Manifest Destiny in bronze and marble. In every case, vantage point and composition were used to unmask pretense. Mount Rushmore was bearable as a reflection in a window at best. Anyone who still doubted that Friedlander's oeuvre was laced with humor and cynicism learned differently here. Nor was he able to face the gravestones at Stagliano cemetery in Genoa, Italy, with anything but irony, using careful cropping to spoof the sentimental poses of mourning on the marble reliefs.

Again and again, Friedlander sought out gardens, parks, and open countryside, though admittedly "great American landscapes" à la Ansel Adams could hardly be expected of him. His favorite motifs were dead or leafless trees, and he was especially fascinated by the graphic textures of dense branches and undergrowth. In the 1990s, the Sonora Desert in Arizona became his ideal landscape. Friedlander also photographed flowerbeds, gardens, and flowers—the last blossomless, reduced to stems in water-filled glass vases.

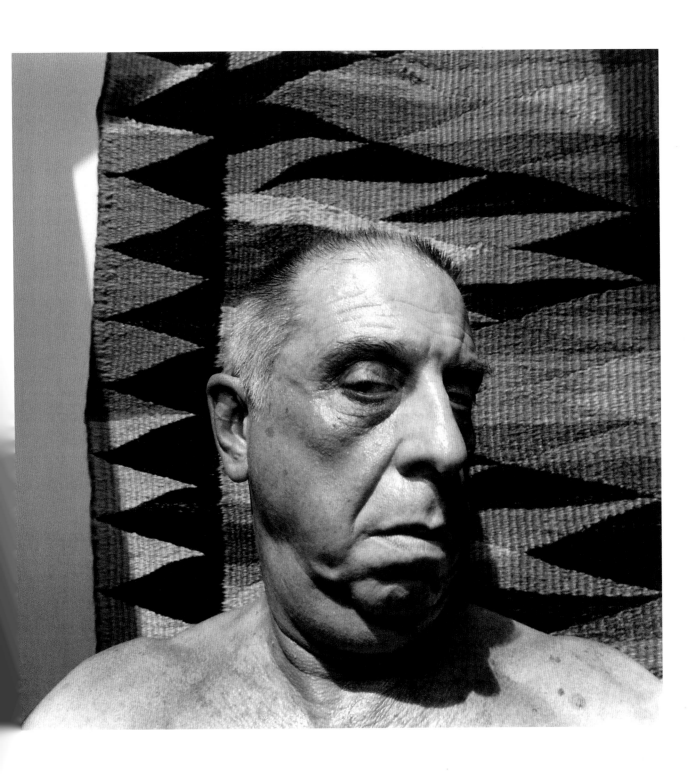

New City, New York, 1997

41

MALICK SIDIBÉ

Sidibé was the party photographer par excellence. He recorded the young people of Mali in West Africa during the euphoria of the post-liberation years. No other photographic archive contains more laughing, dancing, and smiling than that of the international award-winning photographer from Bamako.

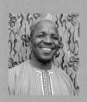

MALICK SIDIBÉ

1936 Born in Soloba, French Sudan, now Mali

1952 Graduates from secondary school

To 1955 Attends the École Nationale des Arts, Bamako, to become a goldsmith, followed by training at the Photographic Service studio run by the Frenchman Gérard Guillat (Gégé)

1956 Gets his first camera

1962 Opens his own studio

1995 Retrospective at Fondation Cartier pour l'art contemporain, Paris

2007 Awarded a Golden Lion, Venice Biennale

2016 Dies in Bamako, Mali

When Mali shook off French colonial rule in 1960, Bamako, like other African capitals, went into raptures. But its young men and women had other reasons to celebrate, too. "The city sets you free," as they were likely the country's first younger generation to realize. Malick Sidibé was on the spot, and he untiringly made use of the opportunity. Going to as many as five parties a night, he often developed his films until sunup, so he could show the prints quickly and take orders for enlargements.

Sidibé must have enjoyed his role immensely. When he turned up at one of the countless parties in nocturnal Bamako, he would actuate his flash, and everyone knew "Malick's here!" In his mid-20 at the time, he was only a little older than his clientele, and completely integrated in this—by now historical—generation.

Fêtes surprises or *fêtes poussières* these events were known as, because the dancing in the unpaved courtyards set the dust flying. Or people congregated at their parents' homes or one of the countless clubs that shot up like mushrooms, and had names that Malick still often uses as picture titles: Happy Boys Club, Lionceaux Club, Beatles Club, and more. This was the era of the twist, cha cha cha, and later rock 'n' roll and beat. A record went on the turntable and the mating game could begin. Cheeky dance steps and poses, fashionable garb and the latest record sleeves set the scene.

Malick captured the spontaneity and charm of these fetes with a fresh eye. He also accompanied his customers down to the banks of the Niger, showing them swimming, rollicking, and just letting off steam. His photographs record the way the sexes were able to meet freely and openly in public for the first time, beyond all traditional West African etiquette. The photographer's informal style corresponded to his subjects' improvisational skill. In addition, Malick ran—and still runs—a classic photographic studio that attracts individuals and couples on a variety of Christian and Islamic holidays, as well as other occasions.

The party days were already over by the 1970s, when increasing socialist regimentation and curfews suffocated Mali's nightlife. For many years Malick had to supplement his income by repairing cameras. It was not until the discovery in the 1990s of his studio and archive that he became known outside Africa.

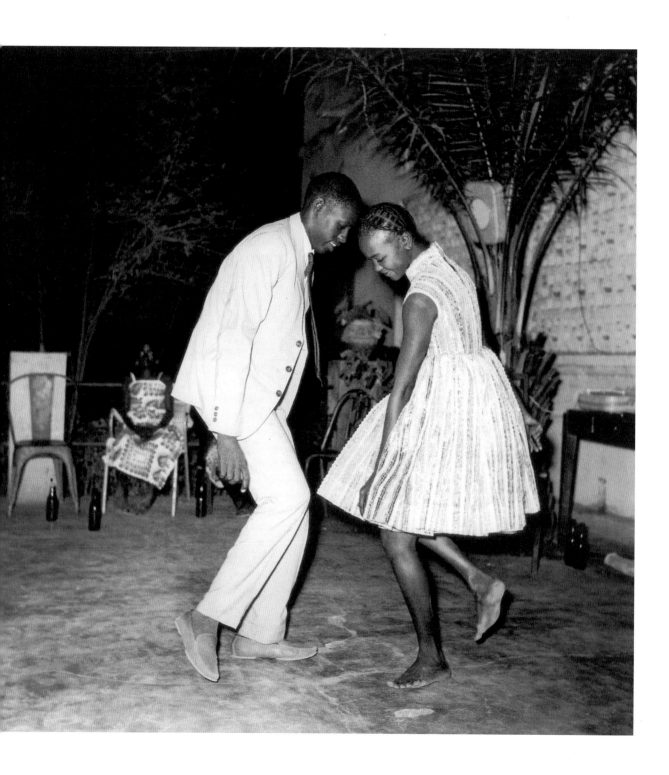

Christmas Eve, 1963

42

JOSEF KOUDELKA

Josef Koudelka's eye was sharpened by the experience of being an outsider. For 15 years he lived a nomad's life, with no permanent residence, "on the minimum," as he later said, and photographed only what interested him.

In his 1988 classic, *Exiles*, Josef Koudelka summed up his vagabond life as a stranger in strange lands. Even randomly observed scenes on streets, in fields, in parks, or on the coast draw meaning from the general context of "exile." In the over 60 images, animals repeatedly appear like leitmotifs—stray dogs, a monkey on a chain, a turtle turned on its back, a dead crow hung on a string. We are continually faced by situations of estrangement, visual and psychological disquiet—parables of human homelessness. Beyond exile in the narrower, political sense, Koudelka brings other associations to the theme. Even tarpaulins dangling from a scaffold, an upturned boat, or sunbathers on the steps of the Metropolitan Museum reverberate with a sense of exile.

Back in 1975, Koudelka published the book that made him famous in the West: *Gypsies*. Avoiding all romantic clichés, he showed Romany families with their children, their living rooms, humble houses, poor settlements. Europe's largest border-crossing ethnic group became visible as a basically closed society with its own heritage and intrinsic quotidian beauty.

From 1986 onwards, Koudelka produced numerous series, especially landscapes, using a panoramic camera: the devastation caused by open-pit mining in northern Bohemia (1990–1994), war-ravaged Beirut (1991), the changing countryside around the Lhoist limestone quarries in the Limelette region of Belgium (2001), the Camargue (2002), and archeological sites in Greece (2003). His panoramic formats were displayed both horizontally and vertically. It was not "beautiful" landscapes that interested him but "landscapes altered by contemporary man." Despite the destructiveness of open-pit mining, Koudelka did not see himself in the role of environmentalist but discovered in such scarred landscapes an "untamed beauty, strength."

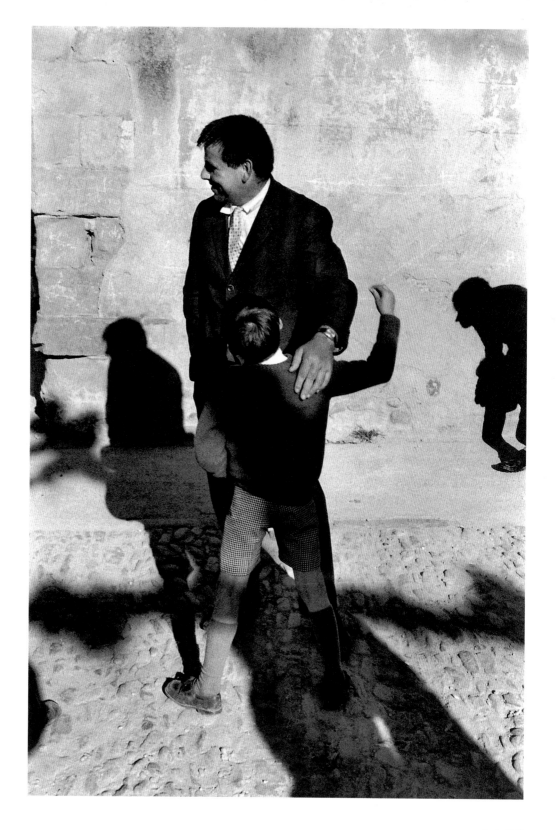

Spain, 1973

43

SEBASTIÃO SALGADO

From the start of his career, Salgado has focused on documenting the burning issues of our time, his study of economics giving him insight into the causes of global crises such as famine, migration, and the spread of slums.

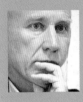

SEBASTIÃO SALGADO

1944 Born in Aimorés, Brazil

1963–1967 Studies economics; works for the Ministry of Finance, Brazil

1969 Studies in Paris

1971–1973 Works for the International Coffee Organization (ICO); takes his first photographs

1973 Documents the famine in the Sahel

1974 Active for the Sygma Agency

1975–1979 Active for the Gamma Agency

1977–1984 Trips to South America

1984–1985 Documents the drought in North Africa

1986 *Sahel: L'Homme en détresse*

1986–1992 *Workers*

1994 Founds Amazonas Images, Paris

2007 *Africa*

Salgado lives in Paris

Sebastião Salgado is the best-known representative of a new brand of photojournalism. Instead of doing one job after another for a magazine or picture agency, he conceives comprehensive photographic projects, complete with sponsoring and logistics, that extend over several years. Exhibitions and publications, including partial publication in magazines, are components of the planning. Initially a member of the photographic agencies Sygma and Gamma, then under contract to Magnum, Salgado later shed all corporate ties to work independently for his own firm, Amazonas Images, headed by his wife, Lélia Wanick Salgado.

During his activity for the Investment Department of the International Coffee Organization (ICO), Salgado already became interested in issues of development policy. He had found the subject of his lifetime; but at 30, he decided to address it from a different angle, through photography. As early as 1973, he took up two of his main themes: famine in the Sahel zone of Africa, and guest workers in Europe. The following years were spent primarily in Latin America—on a search for images of "other Americas." Salgado's travels took him through the Andean countries of Ecuador, Bolivia and Peru, back to his native country, Brazil, and to Guatemala and Mexico, where he spent prolonged periods among the Tarahumara and Mixtecs of Oaxaca. Salgado photographed rural people at their everyday occupations and their festivals. Uninterested in formal experiments, he approached them with empathy and respect.

The years' long drought that hit the African Sahel in the mid 1980s brought an end to rural idylls for Salgado, confronting him with a disaster of immense scope. The images he made for Magnum in Ethiopia, Mali, Chad, and Sudan, later collected in the volume *Sahel: L'Homme en détresse* (Sahel: Man in Distress), are among the most shocking in his oeuvre.

Though known for his earlier books, it was *Workers: An Archaeology of the Industrial Age* (1993) that brought Salgado international fame. It was a homage to working people, "a farewell to a world of manual labor that is slowly disappearing and a tribute to those men and women who still work as they have for centuries," as he wrote in his dedication. The book recorded traditional manual tasks from sugar cane harvesting and cigar manufacturing in Cuba, through tuna fishing in Sicily, to sulfur collecting on Kawah Idjen in Indonesia, and also documented mechanical lead smelting in Kasachstan and oil drilling in Baku, Azerbaijan. The 1986 images of the enormous maw of a gold mine in Serra Pelada, Brazil, with thousands of miners crawling antlike up and down steep ladders, are among the most compelling and disturbing in the entire series.

With the volume *Exodus* (1998), Salgado was one of the first to visually address a key contemporary theme: the worldwide migrations and displacements resulting from wars, economic crises, and political terror. He spent seven years photographing in 39 countries. Whether Mexicans crossing the American border wall, Africans who envisage Spain as an El Dorado, the Boat People of Southeast Asia, or Ruandans who fled to the Congo—in 25 crisis regions Salgado has recorded the extent of the migrations that have become the rule on our planet. No one who discusses this issue in future will be able to do so without remembering Salgado's moving images.

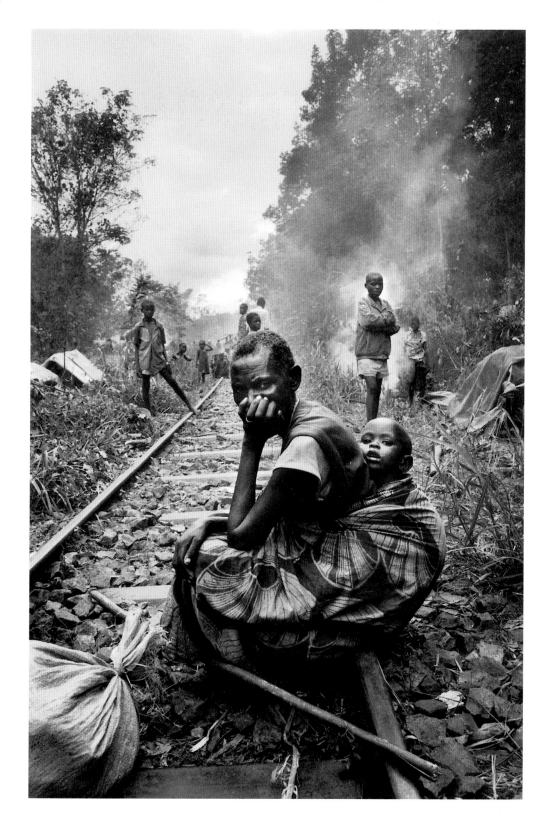

Refugees in the Democratic Republic of the Congo, March 28, 1997

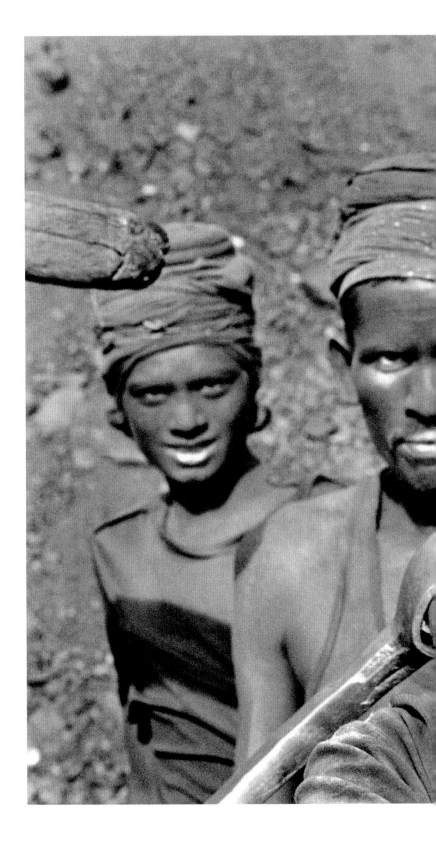

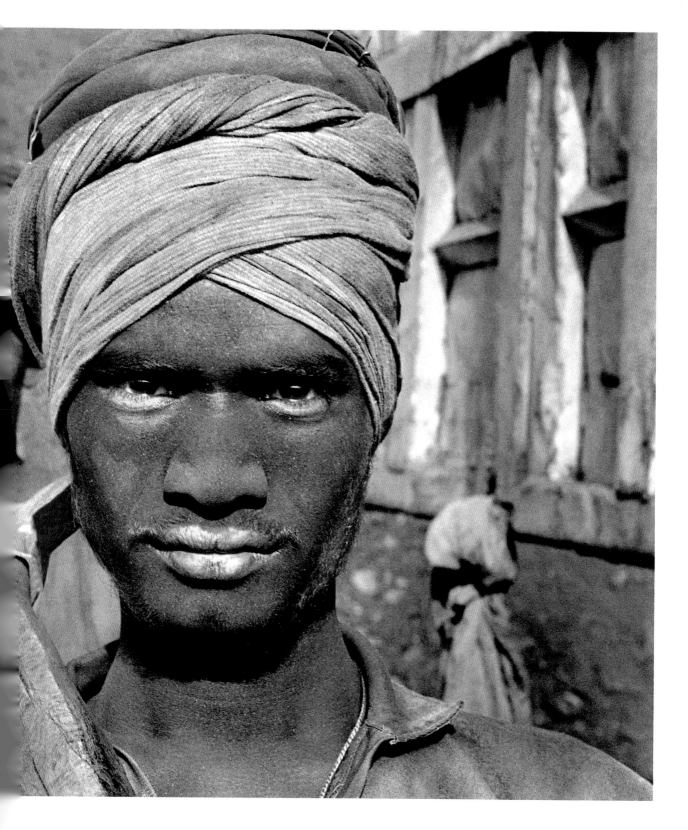

Workers (Women and Men), Dhanbad, Bihar State, India, 1989

44

ROBERT MAPPLETHORPE

Robert Mapplethorpe subjected hard-core sex and the sheer beauty of flowers to the same rigorous aesthetic. Parts of his work amount to a stylized showroom of gay subculture, and at the same time a requiem for a photographer who died of AIDS.

ROBERT MAPPLETHORPE

1946 Born in Queens, New York

1963–1965 Studies advertising design, graphic art, drawing, painting and sculpture at the Pratt Institute, Brooklyn

1967 Meets the rock musician Patti Smith, with whom he will move into the Chelsea Hotel in 1969; works as a show-window decorator

1968 Material collages: boxes, triptychs and "altars," which will later include photographs from porn magazines

1971 Begins using a Polaroid camera

1977 Represented at Documenta, Kassel

1980 *Black Males*

1983 *Lady Lisa Lyon*

1985 *Certain People: A Book of People*; photographs Jan Fabre's performance *The Power of Theatrical Madness* in Antwerp

1986 *A Season in Hell: Rimbaud, Mapplethorpe*; diagnosed with AIDS

1989 Dies in Boston, Massachusetts

After Wilhelm von Gloeden and Wilhelm Plüschow, photographs of male nudes no longer caused much of a stir, yet Robert Mapplethorpe broke the last remaining taboos. The more classical of his compositions still relied on early modern photographers, especially Imogen Cunningham. Legs, backs, feet became sculptural forms in their own right, and throats, navels and nipples took on a monumental effect. But the truly shocking aspect of Mapplethorpe's work came with his perfect stagings of practices including S & M and bondage. Drawing on the iconography of porn, he celebrated it with extreme photographic sophistication—a biting synthesis. Mapplethorpe's models and the sexual practices he pictured evidently reflected his personal preferences. In his photographs of African American men, published in book form in 1980, he took the penis cult to an apex, occasionally stylizing their members into still lifes.

Mapplethorpe's images of flowers are virginal by comparison to the rituals of the sexual underground. As early as 1977, he photographed lilies, tulips, orchids and chrysanthemums, a series expanded in the 1980s by highly refined imagery in color. He marshaled all of his stylistic ambition to lend the blossoms the sublime, fragile look of alabaster.

Mapplethorpe was also in great demand as a portraitist of high society. The archbishop of Canterbury sat for him, as did Arnold Schwarzenegger—in bathing trunks (1976). Especially his portraits of women with complexions like china and eyes like glass reflected a style to the taste of *Harper's Bazaar*. The sculptors Louise Nevelson and Louise Bourgeois stand out from this series as true character heads, as does Mapplethorpe's artistic partner and one-time girlfriend, Patti Smith. There are also many portraits of the world champion in bodybuilding, Lisa Lyon, to whom he devoted a book. Of his male portraits, those of his lover, friend and patron, Sam Wagstaff, of Philip Glass & Robert Wilson (1976), David Hockney and Henry Geldzahler (1976), and William Burroughs (1980–1981) are particularly memorable.

Most compelling of all, though, are his self-portraits, some unabashedly narcissistic, others theatrical, and finally those in which we look into the eyes of an artist who has already succumbed to a sense of imminent death. Mapplethorpe presented himself in leather garb with a switchblade (1983), styled himself a devil or a terrorist with machine gun (1983), or made up like a diva with fur stole (1980). Towards the end, his photographs sometimes included skulls, and in the self-portrait made a few months before his death, he leans on a cane with a carved death's-head grip.

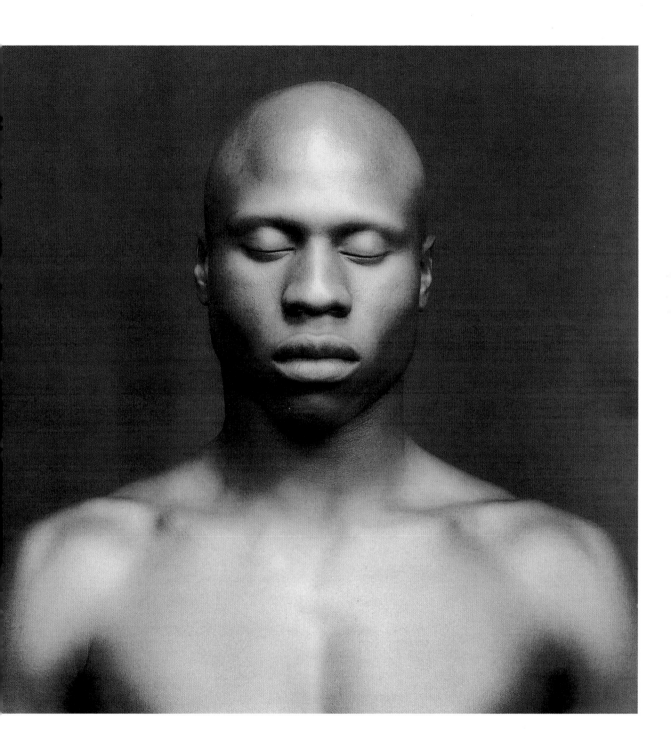

Ken Moody, 1983

45

HIROSHI SUGIMOTO

The Zen master of photography, Hiroshi Sugimoto has taken pictures of empty movie screens, Buddha figures with attributes of equanimity, even colored shadows. He once let the light from burning candles fall through his lens for so long that "the life of a candle" was recorded on film.

HIROSHI SUGIMOTO

What is truly real was revealed to Hiroshi Sugimoto in the American Museum of Natural History in New York, in face of dioramas with crouching Neanderthals and stuffed polar bears on artificial ice floes. Once photographed, he remarked, any object is as good as real.

Nor is water just water. Anyone who thinks a single photograph of the sea says it all is mistaken. Sugimoto set out to photograph every sea and ocean on the planet. In the first year of his *Seascapes* series (1980–2003), it was the Caribbean, seen from Jamaica. Then came the Aegean and the Black Sea, Lake Constance and the Baltic, the North Atlantic, the Sea of Japan, and further bodies of water. Only seasoned sailors have seen as many oceans as Sugimoto. He invariably photographs them from a raised vantage point, with the horizon—now razor sharp, now diffuse—exactly in the middle, and the gently agitated water surface occupying the lower half of the image. Crucial is the large format of 120 x 150 centimeters, which invites contemplation like a window on a world in balance and serenity. He wanted to go back in time to the ancient seas of the world, Sugimoto explained, as a primeval man may have seen them.

A panoply of similar Bodhisattva figures in a 12th-century Kyoto shrine are likewise associated with the sea: *Sea of Buddha* (1995). The faces with closed eyes, contemplating inner boundlessness, exude pure harmony. The associations with Zen are so obvious as to need no explanation. Yet that Sugimoto actually succeeded in projecting the notion of the sheer void into film theaters of the 1920s and 1930s and American drive-in movies is astonishing. The temples of Hollywood illusion were transformed into Zen shrines by leaving the shutter open so long that the crime movies and Westerns on the screen vanished into nothingness. There remained only bright white screens, framed by arabesque decor or the black of the night sky.

In his photographs of mathematical objects, called *Conceptual Forms* (2004), too, Sugimoto strived for pure, absolute form. *Helicoid* or *Hypersphere* are the titles of such depictions of trigonometrical functions, calculated by mathematicians and cast in plaster by master mold-makers. He has also photographed architecture, but with the lens purposely adjusted out of focus. Only really good architecture, the photographer says, can stand up to such "blurring attacks."

As little as Japan would be Japan without the tradition of Samurai violence, no review of Sugimoto's work would be complete without his *Chambers of Horrors*. He spent five years recording the terrors in Madame Tussaud's, from the various methods of execution—guillotine, garrote, hanging, electric chair—to notorious murderers seen in the act. To Sugimoto, these staged scenes seemed more real than the real.

It goes almost without saying that when it came to portraits, contemporaries held little interest for him. He preferred the wax faces of Shakespeare or Emperor Hirohito. An occasion to foreground sumptuous textiles was provided by his series on Henry VIII and his unfortunate wives. Thinking you could go to Sugimoto to have your portrait taken would be to misunderstand the master. You can imagine him politely requesting you to die first and come back in the form of a wax effigy. For Sugimoto, photography contains "great magic," but it is not revealed through a hunt for motifs. It is coaxed out of long exposures that embody "visions in my mind."

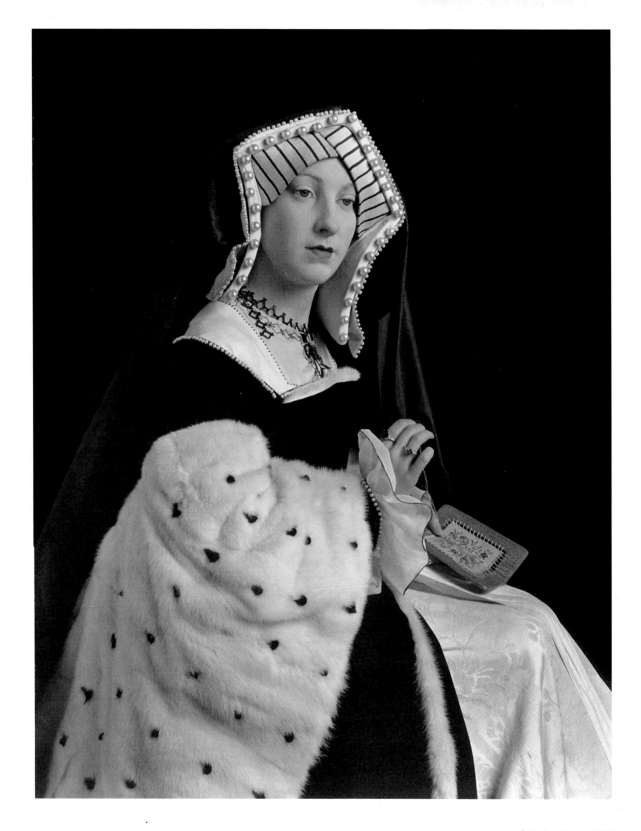

Catherine of Aragon, 1999

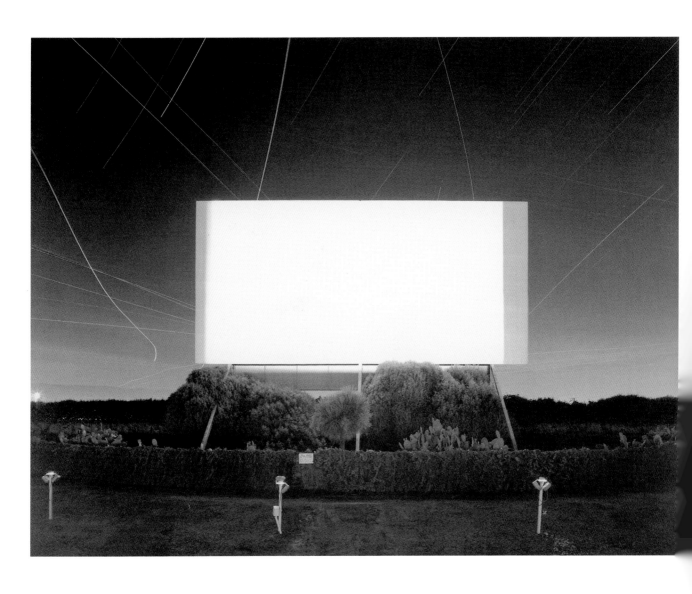

Union City Drive-In, Union City, 1993

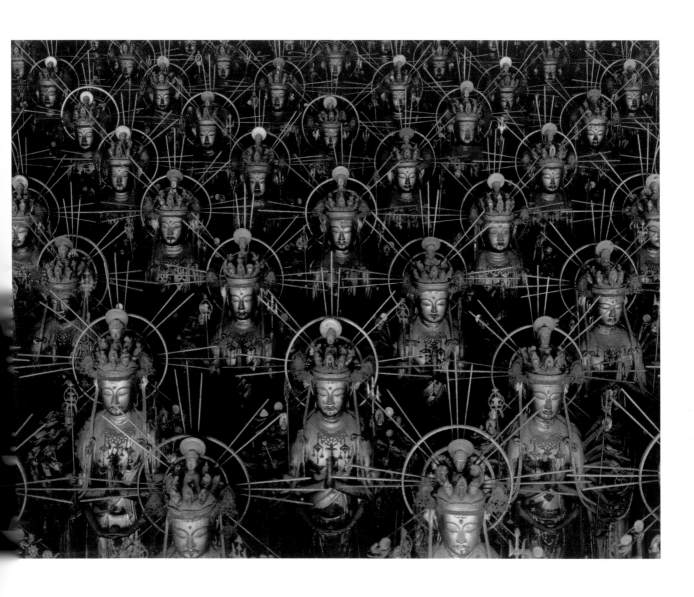

Sea of Buddha, 1995

46

KAVEH GOLESTAN

Kaveh Golestan photographed under two Iranian regimes—that of the Shah, then that of Khomeini, documenting the Islamic Revolution, the Iran-Iraq War, and the Kurdish Revolt. In doing so, he made himself deeply unpopular with the authorities.

KAVEH GOLESTAN

When Queen Farah Diba visited Kaveh Golestan's show *Roospi, Kargaar va Majnoun* in Tehran in 1978, she found his view of life "very gloomy." His photo series on workers, prostitutes in Tehran's Sharh-e No quarter, and children in psychiatric clinics hardly corresponded to the Shah's image of Iran, for which he prescribed modernization and a Western life style.

When Khomeini came to power and some Iranians returned from exile while a million others fled abroad again, when the Shah's feared secret service was replaced by another, religiously orthodox one, reality continued to be selectively defined. The Ayatollahs torched the red light district complete with inhabitants, and fleeing women were strung up on lampposts. Golestan held on for five years before he, too, emigrated with his family to London.

In the meantime, the 1979 winner of the Robert Capa Gold Medal had become internationally known for his pictures of the Iranian Revolution. His famous photograph of the Stars and Stripes, torn from the flagpole of the US Embassy and used by two Shah opponents to tote away their booty, symbolized the end of Iran's orientation to the West, and was published in the *Time Book of the Year*.

Hardly had the gunfire of the revolution died away when the internecine war with Iraq broke out. "I was amazed by how youngsters were willing to die for their beliefs. I felt I had to show this through my photos," Golestan would later write. During the eight years he spent looking "through the camera at death," he captured men dying on stretchers, wounded men swaddled in bandages, and maimed and immolated bodies. Perhaps for one last time a photographer was able to record such unvarnished realities before the embedded journalism of another Iraq war censored them away.

The year the war ended, 1988, saw Iranian Kurdistan rise against the repressive rule of Tehran. At the same time across the border, Saddam Hussein was bombing the Kurdish town of Halabja with poison gas—only the latest, gruesome sign of the social and political oppression under which the Kurds in Iran, Iraq, and Turkey had suffered for centuries. Though himself not a Kurd, Golestan allied himself with these people and their cause. When the West continued to support Saddam, he recorded their desperate resistance. "The subject of my work was death and humanity," Golestan would later sum up his life's work.

In pictures of dances of the Qaderi dervishes in the Zagross Mountains of western Iran, he shed light on quite a different side of Kurdish culture. Singing, praying and dancing to the beat of great tambourines, the Sufis whirled themselves into a trance, an ecstatic confrontation with God—scenes no tourist but only a true friend was permitted to witness.

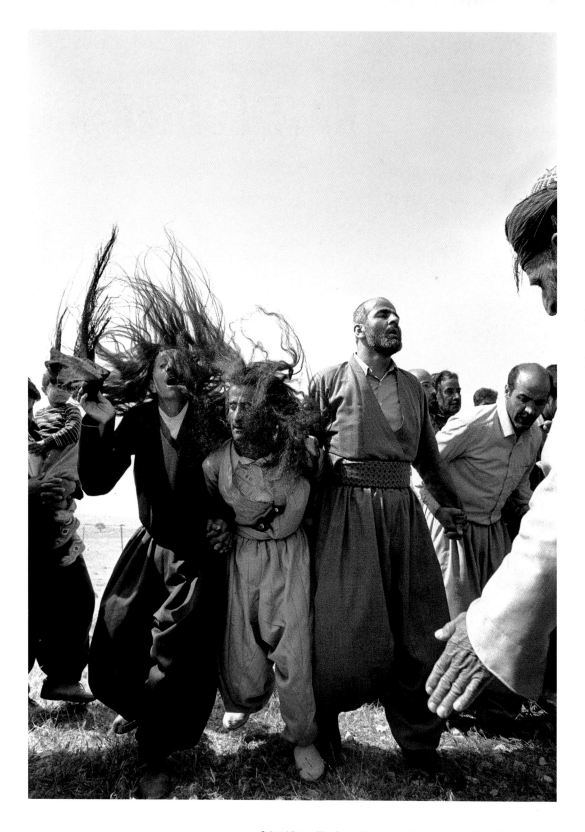

Spirutal Dance (The Qaderi Dervishes of Kurdistan, Zagros Mountains series), 1990

47

MARTIN PARR

Martin Parr's dry wit and inventiveness have enliven a field that seems commercial sterile. Yet he is not afraid of boredom and bad taste—they are the source of his art's true strength.

MARTIN PARR

1952 Born in Epsom, England

1970–1973 Studies photography at Manchester Polytechnic

1972 Photo series *Butlin's by the Sea*

1976–1977 *Beauty Spots*

1980–1983 *A Fair Day*

1982 *Bad Weather*

1986 *The Last Resort: Photographs of New Brighton*

1989 *The Cost of Living*

1993 *Bored Couples* and *Home and Abroad*

1996 *Prefabs*

1999 *Common Sense, Benidorm,* and *Boring Postcards*

2000 *Think of England*

2003 *Bliss: Postcards of Couples and Families*

2016 *Unseen City*

He put on a bored face every time he let himself be snapped in colleagues' studios, or with a stuffed baby lion in the MGM Grand Hotel in Las Vegas, or vanishing into the maw of a shark in Benidorm, Spain. He couldn't have found it easy to suppress a smile. Boredom seems to have had a magical attraction for Martin Parr ever since 1977–1978, when he recorded scenes from small Methodist communities in Yorkshire, and 1981, when he photographed the series *Bad Weather*. Then he commenced collecting "boring postcards" from the 1930s and 1940s. Subsequently, he invested considerable effort in making 468 pictures of all the streets, houses and stores in the town of Boring, Oregon, USA (2000). Another series was devoted solely to bored couples.

His early photographs, distantly reminiscent of Robert Doisneau, occasionally have an ironic undertone, as when the guests at *The Mayor of Todmorden's Inaugural Banquet* in Yorkshire threaten to stab each other with their forks (1977). The comfy tastelessness of British sitting-rooms and bedrooms has intrigued him from the start.

At 30, Parr turned to color photography, a hurdle he took with ease. In *Tupperware Party, Salford, Greater Manchester* (1985), the red of the plastic contributed greatly to the tragicomic mood of the scene. From here on, the garish colors of commercial merchandise never let him go. For the series *One Day Trip* (1983–1986), Parr accompanied fellow Britons on their buying sprees to the supermarkets of Boulogne, France. The mountains of goods piled in teetering shopping carts are a festival of acrid color. A contrast is provided by his shots of families in the age of Margaret Thatcher, on Sunday outings to dingy bathing resorts near Liverpool, where the waste heaps abound.

When in 1995 Parr switched from medium format to 35 mm and used a ring flash in daylight to illuminate every pore of his sitters' faces, his sarcasm and the color temperature of his images reached boiling point. The shrill colors made the banality of the close-ups well-nigh unbearable. In the series *Think of England*, begun in the late 1990s, he showed his countrymen sunbathing, their bellies either already filled or just being topped off with a greasy bacon sandwich. From aristocratic receptions to snack bars, Parr wended his way through the most diverse of milieus. Benidorm, a tourist grill on the hotel-lined Costa Blanca firmly in the hands of British tourists, provided Parr with a sunburn red that formed a surreal contrast to the hues of towels and sea. Cheap consumption was paralleled by the cheap laser prints used to reproduce the pictures of *Common Sense* and other series, which were sent—"ugly, colorful and bright"—touring around the world in dozens of exhibitions.

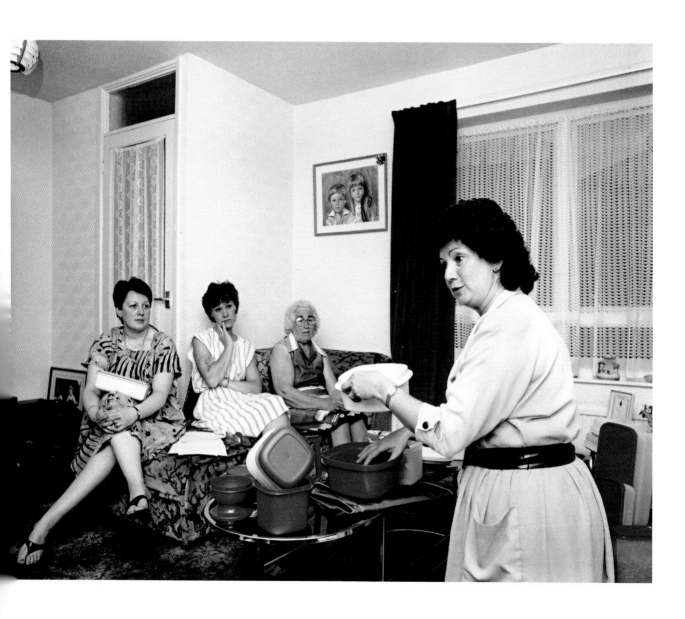

GB. England. Greater Manchester. Salford. A Tupperware party. From *Home and Abroad*, 1986

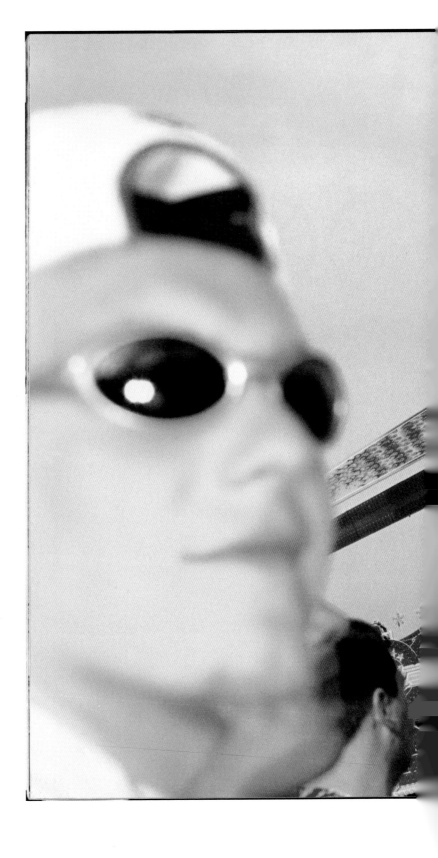

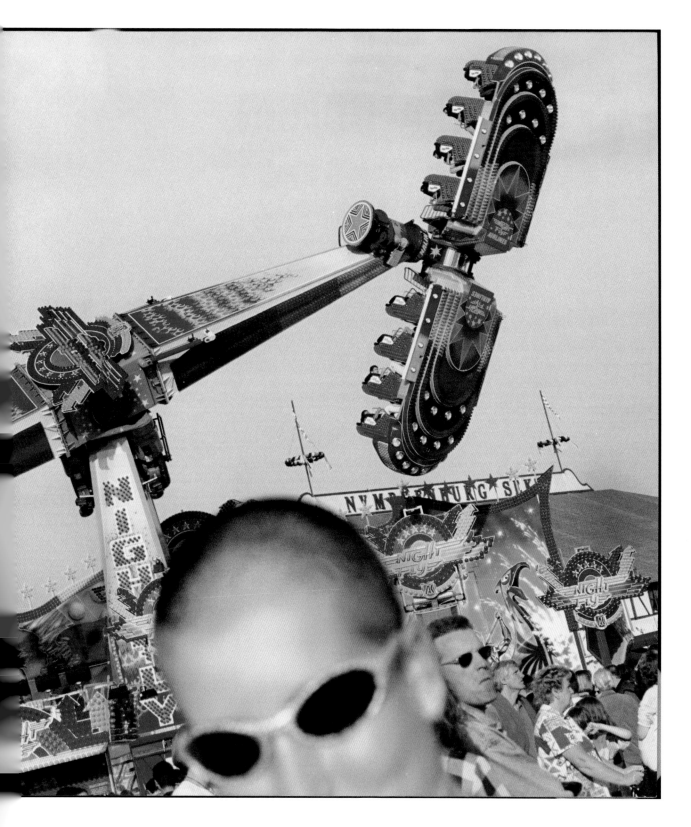

Oktoberfest, Munich, 1997

48

NAN GOLDIN

With Nan Goldin, even the most intimate things appear in public, on high-gloss Cibachrome. These are "snapshots out of love," a desire to remember people, places, times, as she herself says.

Having grown up in the gay scene, the subculture of drag queens, junkies and their milieu is homeground to Nan Goldin. New York, late 1970s—the scene establishes itself on the Lower East Side, where the rents have plummeted. Nightlife burgeons in the lofts and clubs, they dance until they drop at the Mudd Club, TR 3, Isaiah's, awash in alcohol. Existentialism with an American twist. Warhol's films inspire Goldin to take private life seriously, aesthetically. Though she would love to make films herself, she just keeps on making personal photographs like she had as a teenager. Her flash sheds garish light on scenes in bars, lofts and clubs, in her own living room and bedroom—rumpled beds, people embracing, having sex, in front of the mirror, in the bathtub, on a train. She portrays her countless friends, on a search for themselves somewhere between masculine and feminine or both at once. Nan's eye, as Luc Sante noted, could search out the dirtiest corners of a dingy apartment and discover colors and textures no one else had ever seen—sunset oranges, oceanic blues, hellish, seductive reds. We experience the people close to Goldin laughing and crying, in their loneliness as in their comforting togetherness. Or as they contract AIDS, go through phases of recovery, then mostly, inevitably, succumb. *Gotscho Kissing Gilles, Paris* (1993) is probably one of the most moving records of this theme, because it reflects profound emotional involvement. Many of Goldin's photographs form parts of a requiem, many of her friends having died young.

Then there are her self-portraits, many of them—alone, in an embrace with someone she loves, with black eyes after being beaten by her lover, clean after having broken her drug habit in 1988, or in the hospital after an accident.

At some point Goldin began to project her slides on the walls of clubs: a "family album" in which everybody recognized everybody else. Later she underscored the show, which ran for several years, with music, and called it *The Ballad of Sexual Dependency*. The selection of pictures continually changed.

Goldin's imagery revealed souls, as Luc Sante wrote, as if she looked through the eyes of the people she photographed in both directions. She showed her life, in which her friends and partners played the starring role.

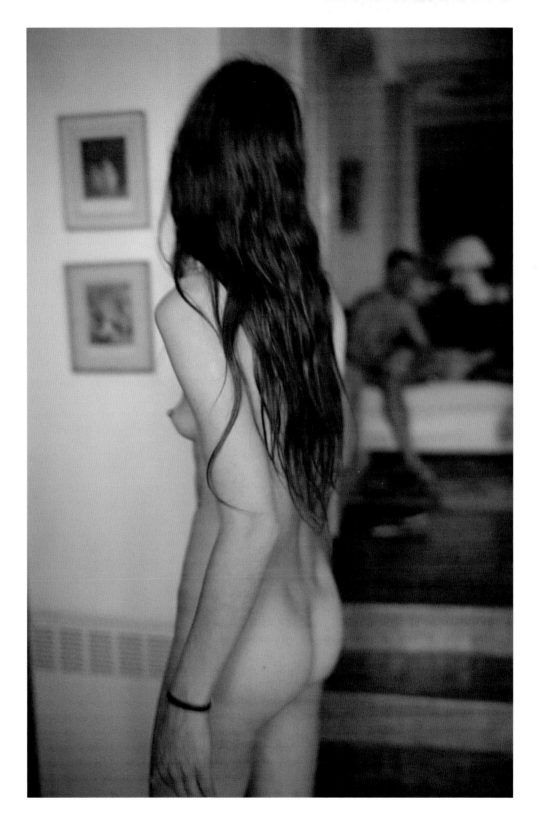

Joana's Back in the Doorway, Chateauneuf de Gadagne, Avignon 2000

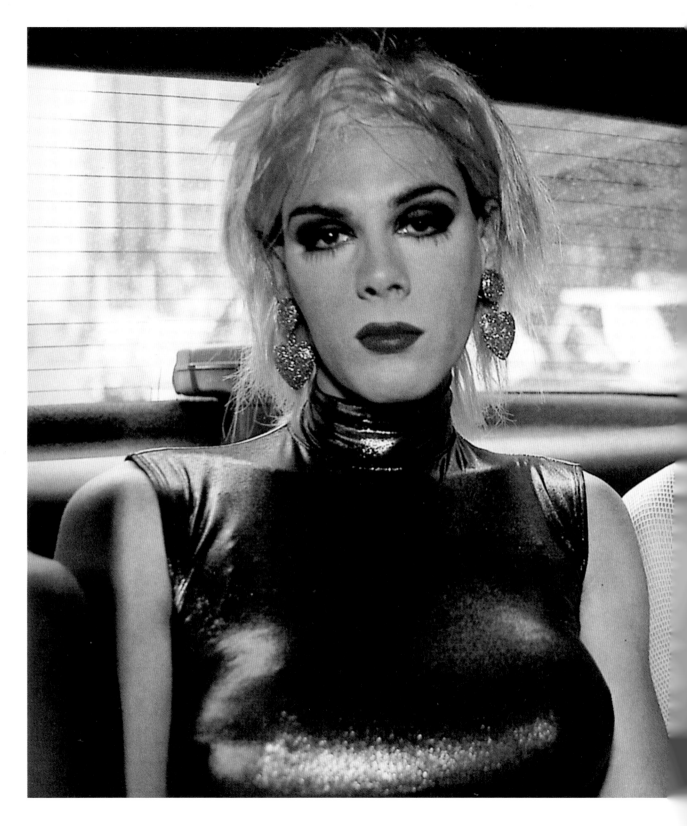

Misty and Jimmy Paulette in a Taxi, NYC, 1991

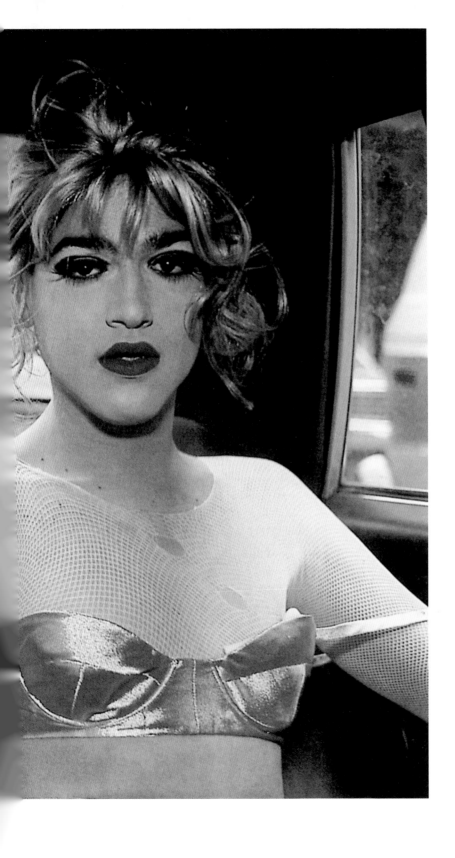

49

ANDREAS GURSKY

The aesthetic of Google Earth and mass scenes à la Hollywood inform the work of this shooting star on the photography scene, who draws record prices on the international art photo market.

ANDREAS GURSKY

1955   Born in Leipzig, Germany

1978–1981   Studies at the Folkwang School, Essen

1981–1987   Studies at the Düsseldorf Art Academy, with Bernd Becher

1989   Exhibition at the Centre Genevois de Gravure Contemporaine, Geneva; 303 Gallery, New York; Museum Haus Lange, Krefeld

1994   *Andreas Gursky, Photographs 1984–1993*, exhibition at the Deichtorhallen, Hamburg, and De Appel Stichting, Amsterdam

2001   Exhibition at MoMA, New York

2007   Exhibition at the Haus der Kunst, Munich

2008   Exhibitions at Istanbul Museum of Modern Art, Istanbul

2015   Museum Frieder Burda, Baden-Baden, Germany

Andreas Gursky lives in Düsseldorf

Whether the current triumphs of young photographers are more the result of the demise of painting, a hunger for realistic imagery, or a variant of the proliferating "overdesign" of life and art, is something only time will tell. What we can say is that photographers no longer lack self-confidence, and that their gigantic glossy formats are stealing the show from contemporary painting. In retrospect, images by Albert Renger-Patzsch or Henri Cartier-Bresson look like miniatures. These masters refused to be called artists. Andreas Gursky, in contrast, would feel insulted if one referred to him as a photographer, in the craft sense. Like the German photographers Axel Hütte, Jörg Sasse, Thomas Struth, Candida Höfer, and Thomas Ruff, Gursky was a student of the Bechers.

Gursky's works are visual symphonies, obsessively packed with detail of a *trompe l'œil* precision. Like Albrecht Altdorfer's monumental painting *Alexander's Victory*, each of his subjects is expanded into a spatially all-encompassing universal landscape.

His *Tour de France I* (2007) shows an Alpine stage that effortlessly covers two vertical kilometers in altitude. An asparagus field in *Beelitz* (2007), seen in a bird's-eye view, rises into a linear pattern that recalls the slats of a ventilation duct. The archipelago of Gursky's *James Bond Island* seems to consist of all the islands in Micronesia.

Gursky's images tempt us to search for the joints between the separate pictures of which they are composed and the hinges between their changes of perspective. His reproduction of modules of a motif present intriguing rebuses to the eye. The photographic illusions and cinematic effects are fascinating: mass scenes reminiscent of the movie *Ben Hur (Pyongyang I, 2007)*, or human figures swarming like insects over megastructures à la *Blade Runner* (*Klitschko*, 1999; *Madonna I*, 2001). The stadiums, arenas, factories overflow with people. And then, in sharp contrast, are those images that veritably celebrate aseptic emptiness: *Prada II* (1997), *Schiphol* (1994), or *Supernova* (1999), evoking outer space as the last exit for mankind. This division between puristic places of contemplation—*Rhine II* (1999)—and orgies of global hypertension and mass entertainment—the Chicago stock exchange, the Berlin Love Parade, traffic chaos in Cairo—seems almost schizophrenic. Seen from a great distance, Gursky's crowds appear tame and manageable. Images of mass animal raising in the United States and Japan provide an ironic commentary.

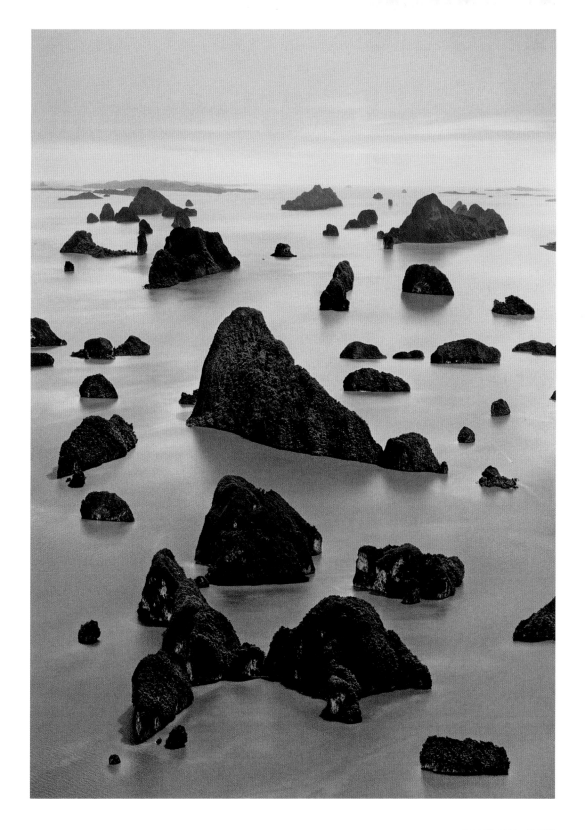

James Bond Island I, 2007

50

WOLFGANG TILLMANS

Wolfgang Tillmans focuses as much on socks draped on a radiator, underarm hair, and naked lovers as he does on abstract color fields and starry skies. He is both hedonistic and committed.

WOLFGANG TILLMANS

1968 Born in Remscheid, Germany

1987–1990 Lives and works in Hamburg

1990–1992 Studies at Bournemouth and Poole College of Art and Design, Bournemouth, UK

1992–1994 Lives and works in London

1994–1995 Lives in New York

1995 Ars Viva Prize, Germany Kunstpreis der Böttcherstraße, Bremen

1996–2007 Lives in London

1998–1999 Visiting professorship at the Hochschule für bildende Künste, Hamburg

2000 Turner Prize, Tate Britain, London

2001 Honorary Fellowship at The Arts Institute at Bournemouth, UK

2003–2009 Professorship of interdisciplinary art at Städelschule, Frankfurt am Main

Since 2006 Exhibition space *Between Bridges*, until 2011 in London, since 2013 in Berlin

From 2011 Lives in London and Berlin

2009–2014 Artist Trustee on the Board of Tate, London

Since 2013 Member of the Royal Academy of Arts, London

A breakfast tray on the folding table on an American Airlines seat is provocatively garnished by the exposed penis of Tillmans' traveling companion. This is one of his many still lifes that consist of flowers, vegetables, underpants, undershirts, or other equally banal things, arranged to bring out their color contrasts. A party-devastated interior complete with scattered leftovers and waste, skillfully illuminated, becomes a feast for the eye. Not even slush dotted with the footprints of passersby escapes Tillmans' lens. In his *paper drops* (2001), he approaches a formal purism that recalls the New Vision of the 1920s.

Again and again Tillmans has turned his attention to people, beginning with pictures of nightlife in London clubs. The approaches of Andy Warhol, Nan Goldin, or Larry Clark may have encouraged him to focus on his friends and private milieu. A series of portraits resulted, and even the commissioned ones retained a personal, intimate character.

Then there is the Tillmans who records cloud formations, manipulates their colors, or draws veils over them (*intervention pieces*), the creator of ethereal images of hair-fine lines on a light ground (*Freischwimmer*) or of dust particles on toned backgrounds (*Silvers*). In other series he conceptually celebrates the intensity of various color and monochrome C-prints, made without a camera. An enthusiastic amateur astronomer from boyhood, Tillmans recorded the Venus transit of June 8, 2004, in sublime photographs.

This is someone who retains freedom of choice of motifs, and continually rediscovers people, things, and situations with an unbiased eye. A cup of tea with a film of grease on it, mice creeping out of the sewer at night... Tillmans effortlessly overcomes the conventional borderlines between genres, including that between "art" and photography.

His exhibitions generally take the form of large-area arrangements of glass-framed C-prints and freely suspended inkjet prints of various format, with purposely disparate motifs and subjects, distributed along the walls according to a momentary whim. In addition, he presents exhibitions as "polyphonal processes," comprising newspaper cuttings, photocopies, and photographs on wooden tables under glass. These reflect the politically conscious and engaged side of Tillmans' nature. Religious terror (*Memorial for the Victims of Organized Religions*, 2006), an inhuman economy dictated by shareholder value, homophobia and AIDS are themes that especially concern him.

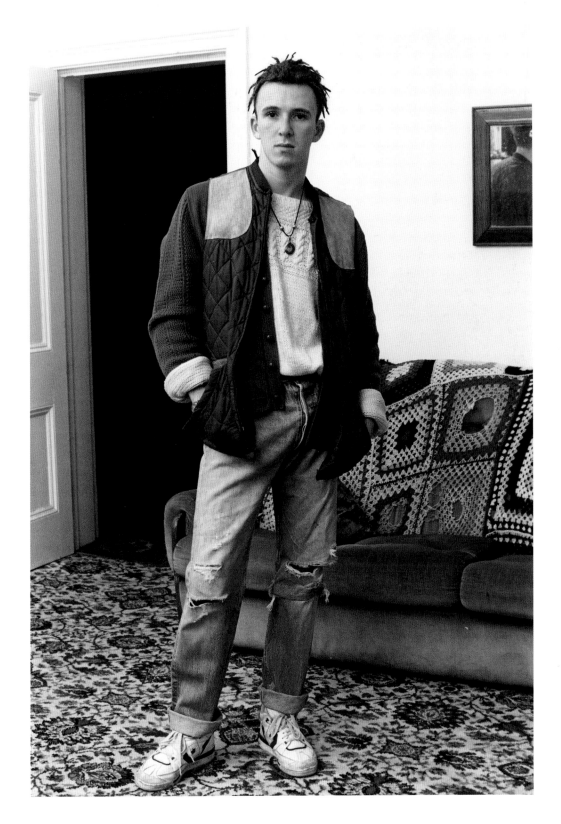

Adam, 1991

PORTRAIT ILLUSTRATIONS

© Prestel Verlag, Munich · London · New York 2016
A member of Verlagsgruppe Random House GmbH, Neumarkter Strasse 28 · 81673 Munich

In respect to links in the book, Verlagsgruppe Random House expressly notes that no illegal content was discernible on the linked sites at the time the links were created. The Publisher has no influence at all over the current and future design, content or authorship of the linked sites. For this reason Verlagsgruppe Random House expressly disassociates itself from all content on linked sites that has been altered since the link was created and assumes no liability for such content.

Prestel Publishing Ltd.
14-17 Wells Street
London W1T 3PD

Prestel Publishing
900 Broadway, Suite 603
New York, NY 10003

Library of Congress Control Number: 2017942342

A CIP catalogue record for this book is available from the British Library.

Editorial direction: Adeline Henzschel in cooperation with Weiß-Freiburg GmbH
Copyediting: Chris Murray and Patrick Müller
Picture editing: Sarah Kempff (Weiß-Freiburg GmbH)
Cover design: Sofarobotnik
Design: normal industries, Munich
Typesetting: Weiß-Freiburg GmbH
Production management: Corinna Pickart
Separations: Reproline Mediateam, Munich
Printing and binding: DZS Grafik, d.o.o., Ljubljana
Paper: Profimatt

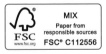

MIX
Paper from responsible sources
FSC® C112556
www.fsc.org

Verlagsgruppe Random House FSC® N001967

Printed in Slowenia

ISBN 978-3-7913-8359-0

www.prestel.com

LEWIS W. HINE
1874–1940

AUGUST SANDER
1876–1964

EDWARD STEICHEN
1879–1973

EDWARD WESTON
1886–1958

MAN RAY
1890–1976

PAUL STRAND
1890–1976

ALEXANDER RODCHENKO
1891–1956

ANDRÉ KERTÉSZ
1894–1985

JULIA MARGARET CAMERON
1815–1879

JACQUES-HENRI LARTIGUE
1894–1986

FÉLIX NADAR
1820–1910

DOROTHEA LANGE
1895–1965

MATHEW BRADY
1823–1896

EUGÈNE ATGET
1857–1927

JOSEF SUDEK
1896–1976

EADWEARD JAMES MUYBRIDGE
1830–1904

ALFRED STIEGLITZ
1864–1946

ALBERT RENGER-PATZSCH
1897–1966

FELICE BEATO
CA. 1834–1907/1908

EDWARD SHERIFF CURTIS
1868–1952

BRASSAÏ
1899–1984

1810–1830s   1840–1860s   1870–1890s

TIMELINE